INN AND AROUND
NEDERLAND
ACCOMMODATING THE TRAVELER
THEN AND NOW

by Silvia Pettem

© 1998
Tourism and Recreation Program
of Boulder County, Inc. (TARP)

All rights reserved.

Peak to Peak Series #2
ISBN 1-891274-01-5

Others in the Series --
Excursions From Peak to Peak, Then and Now
by Silvia Pettem

On the front cover is an 1899 photo of the Gold Miner Hotel in Eldora. Courtesy Elmer Holmes. On the back cover is Dick's Service Station in Nederland, ca. 1940s. Carnegie Branch Library for Local History, Boulder.

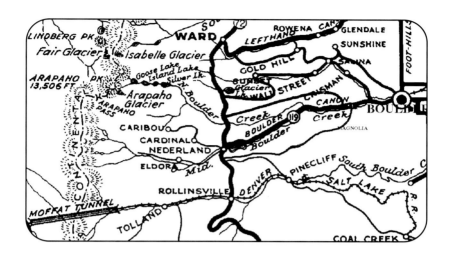

The "Inn and Around Nederland" area extends from Ward to Rollinsville and from Magnolia to Caribou. This book is written to give an impression of the history of the area but is not meant to be all-inclusive.

Nederland is reached by Colorado 119 and Colorado 72 from the south, Colorado 119 from the east, and Colorado 72 from the north.

This map is based on a Boulder Chamber of Commerce map from 1946.

I wish to thank several people who contributed to this book. They include Alice Cross Anderson, Barbara Bolton, Earl Bolton, Diane Brown, Scott Bruntjen, Glenna Carline, Roberta Childers, Jody Corruccini, Wendy Hall, Elmer Holmes, Jean Kindig, Mary Jo Reitsema, and Carol Rinderknecht, as well as the late Isabel Hansen Cross and Helen "D." Dunnagan.

*Financial assistance was provided by
the Goldminer Hotel and the
Boulder County Commissioners.*

CONTENTS

Introduction	1
Nederland and the Silver in Caribou	7
Nederland and the Gold in Eldora	19
Eldora's Gold Rush	23
The Gold Miner Hotel	29
Eldora After the Boom	35
Tourists Discover Eldora	41
Train to the Top of the World	51
Magnolia and Upper Boulder Canyon	63
Ward Wakes Up	69
Rebirth of Nederland	81
Nederland's Tungsten Boom	89
Eldora Through the Years	107
In Conclusion	117
Books on the Nederland Area	120
Index	122

Darwin Andrews and H. N. Wheeler posed with their burro alongside Barker Meadows, below Nederland. This photograph was taken in 1898, a decade before the beginning of the construction of Barker Dam. Carnegie Branch Library for Local History, Boulder Historical Society collection.

INTRODUCTION

"It's easy to get excited about the register of an old hotel in a booming mining camp," wrote author and historian Forest Crossen many years ago when he examined the ledger books for the Antler's Hotel in Nederland. "It is the record of the restless ones, stalwart adventurers from far places in search of quick fortune and excitement, lovely young women destined to follow some of these adventurers to the end, wives coming out to join husbands, children seeing their fathers after years of absence, and the curious — always the curious."

Inns were necessary for traveling salesmen, mining investors, or even an occasional reporter. Tourists existed, but were few and far between in the early days. Unlike Estes Park or Manitou Springs, the Nederland area was not a sophisticated resort or health spa. Generally, accommodations were practical, and their availability ebbed and flowed along with the economic situations of the times.

Let your curiosity be your guide as you explore the area in and around Nederland. Try to put yourself in the place of a late nineteenth century or early twentieth century traveler to one or more of the mountain towns. Imagine the old buildings as they smelled of fresh lumber and glistened with their first coat of paint.

If you could go back in time you would find that the food

was good and ample provisions were made for your horse. Your hosts gave you a hearty welcome and were eager for news from outside their own towns. Most of the people were hard-working businessmen and women trying to make an honest living. Of course there were a few who didn't fit in. Overall, they were no different than people today.

THE UTES

Even before gold prospectors arrived in what became Colorado, explorers and mountain men trapped and traded on their own and mingled quietly with the Utes. West of Lake Eldora, at timberline, the late Wesley Hetzer found a "straight line of rocks about a half-mile long." He related in a 1946 interview that an old-timer, Oran Beach, told him the rocks were part of the Ute trail from Boulder to Rollins Pass.

According to Beach, the Indians tried to cross the pass on horseback one winter, but the snow was so deep they couldn't get through. They returned to the Beach ranch, east of Eldora at Sulphide Flats, picked up rocks, rode back up, and dropped them in the snow. Finally, after several trips, they had built up the trail and made it passable, then continued on to Middle Park.

Hetzer, a longtime Nederland resident, rode the trail several times and said it was easily-recognizable for thirty or forty years.

Author Donald Kemp, who spent parts of his childhood in Eldora during its early days, discovered many Indian artifacts. Kemp wrote that he and his friends often stumbled upon campsites complete with flint arrowheads and spearheads used by the Indians.

THE COLORADO GOLD RUSH

In the early 1850s, most of the overland gold seekers on their way to the California gold rush crossed South Pass in Wyoming in order to avoid the "barrier" of the central Rocky Mountains. Only a few adventurers went out of their way to "look for color" along the Front Range. Among them was Green Russell with a band of Cherokees from Georgia.

A few years later, the East was in the midst of a Depression called the "panic of 1857." Banks were closed, credit was unobtainable, and many people were in financial distress. What was needed was another gold rush closer to home. In 1858, after Russell returned to what is now the Denver area and found "pay dirt," the "Pike's Peak gold rush" was on.

At the time, the fortieth parallel (now Baseline Road in Boulder) divided the western parts of Kansas and Nebraska Territories. When news of Russell's find reached the midwestern newspapers, reporters announced a fortune to be made in the "Kansas gold fields." Instead of asking "Why go?" many men, mostly single, simply said, "Why not?"

In the fall of 1858, a small party of prospectors broke off from the others as they followed the Platte River to the Denver area. At Fort St. Vrain, now Platteville, the group headed west and camped at the mouth of Boulder Canyon (originally spelled Canon), then part of Nebraska Territory. The men named their townsite Boulder City, then prospected in the mountains. Soon they found promising quantities of gold in Gold Run, a creek near Gold Hill. The men panned and sluiced the creek waters, then began the harder task of underground mining.

 Although the Kansas-Nebraska Act of 1854 claimed this land for the federal government and solemnly guaranteed it to the Indians, the miners chose to stay. Since no government existed at all in the western part of the territories, the men formed their own districts. Early in 1859 Gold Hill was known as Mountain District #1, Nebraska Territory, and became the first governing body in what would become Colorado.

Ward, named after early prospector Calvin Ward, became another early gold mining district. One of its first important mines was the Columbia. By the mid-1860s, two hundred people were said to have lived in the town. They had tidy frame houses, one water-powered and five steam-powered stamp mills, and enough wild raspberries for the whole population.

The stamp mills consisted of large iron cylinders which rose and fell night and day and literally stamped, or crushed, the gold ore. However, the early mills were equipped to handle only the high-grade surface ores. When these ores were exhausted and unoxidized ores needed refining, the old mills became useless. The most productive mining and milling years of Gold Hill and Ward were still to come.

GRAND ISLAND MINING DISTRICT

By 1861, the year that both Boulder County and Colorado Territory were created, several other mining districts had been formed. Among them was Grand Island which extended from Castle Rock in Boulder Canyon to the top of the Continental Divide. Supposedly, the prospectors in this area came across a mountain with streams on both sides and said of the mountain, "It looks like a big grand island."

The *Colorado Business Directory* for 1871 stated, "Grand Island takes its name from a beautiful mountain, surrounded by the waters of the North Boulder, containing an area of seventy-five acres, covered with luxuriant grasses and forests of mountain pines, which rises about five hundred feet above a fine park (formerly Trannemaker's, now Hill's ranch), five miles from the main range and fifteen miles from Boulder City. About one mile above the island the North Boulder, a considerable stream, furnishing superior water power, escapes its mountain confines through a deep canon in a spur of the main range; here its waters divide, wind around the mountain, and again unite in the beautiful valley beyond."

Hill's Ranch became Caribou Ranch, and the area to its west is surrounded by the North Boulder and one of its tributaries. Perhaps this land is the legendary "Grand Island."

MIDDLE BOULDER

No one knows who was the first to arrive in the town which was called Middle Boulder and then became Nederland. By 1861, a "nondescript huddle of cabins along the north side of Middle Boulder Creek" was known as "Dayton." Among its first settlers was Nathan Brown, described by author and historian Geneva Meyring as a "tall, sinewy man with a slight stoop and a bald head." He was given the nickname of "Bolly" which had something to do with his baldness.

Brown built his Mountain House Hotel in approximately 1870, but didn't stay around for long. During an epidemic three of his four children died of diphtheria within one week. Shortly afterwards his wife Caroline filed for divorce. Often Brown was hounded by creditors, and occasionally he ended up in court for disturbing the peace. He eventually sold out and moved to Boulder. Others took over the management of the inn.

The little town of Dayton then became known as "Brown's

Crossing." It was on the wagon road which connected the gold mines of Ward with the mills and smelter at Black Hawk. In 1871 townspeople and a few ranchers needed a central location to pick up their mail. A post office was established, and the town's name was changed to "Middle Boulder" after the stream running through the town.

Middle Boulder, which eventually became Nederland, owes its early prosperity to its location at the intersection of the roads between Ward and Black Hawk and between Boulder and Caribou. The town's growth was affected by the mining of three types of minerals — the silver strike in Caribou, then gold discoveries in Eldora, and finally, in the twentieth century, the enormous production of tungsten.

NEDERLAND AND THE SILVER IN CARIBOU

Middle Boulder might have remained a small quiet community if it were not for the mining camp of Caribou, five miles to the west. The Caribou and Poor Man mines, discovered in 1869, created tremendous excitement and a stampede to the region in 1870. A city of tents clung to the mountainside as the men staked and promoted their claims. Nearly every day they hauled tons of rich silver ore to Nathaniel Hill's recently-opened smelter in Black Hawk.

Stagecoaches brought in an estimated one hundred people per day. By September, 1870, Caribou City was platted. Carpenters were already hard at work. With the approach of winter, a population of 460 settled into substantial frame buildings. The earliest businesses included a grocery store, meat market, billiard parlor, saloon, and boarding house. The Central City *Register* reported, "A Keno house is kept running nightly to relieve honest miners of their troublesome surplus of greenbacks and to give work to the grand jury at its next sitting at Boulder City." The newspaper also stated, "There are at present neither doctors, lawyers, preachers, nor school, though the presence of a score of youngsters shows a great need of the latter."

The frontier mining camp of Caribou never became a tourist resort, yet it wasn't without its hotels. The first to open was the Planter's House, and promoted as follows —

"If you or any of your friends want to visit and enjoy a pleasant place and a good hotel, come to Caribou and stop at the Planter's House, C. Wilkins, proprietor. We are willing to assert that the table of the Planter's House is as neat and tasty, and, proportioned to our location, holds just as many and as well-cooked 'goodies' as any hotel table in Colorado. The building is, perhaps, not as convenient as its lessees desire. But Mr. and Mrs. Wilkins are talking of building a new hotel. If they do, we know it will be the best in Colorado. If you shouldn't happen to believe it, come and see us."

It's not known what happened to the Wilkinses or their enthusiasm, but, by 1874, the proprietor of the Planter's House was William O. Logue, former steamboat engineer and captain in the Union Army. He had previously operated a hotel in Black Hawk. A traveler described the building as "an imposing structure, two-and-a-half stories high, with sleeping, sitting, and dining rooms, plus a ladies' parlor." He added, "The accommodation and fare at this house exceeded my expectations. I found an ample supply of good things, well-ordered and served, and no room left for complaint of want of attention and variety."

Best known of the Caribou hotels was the three-story Sherman House, formally opened with a grand ball for sixty couples on a rainy evening in July, 1875. The hotel had twenty-eight guest rooms, a reading room, parlor, and large dining room. An on-the-scene reporter commented on its "carpeted floors, black walnut furnishings, and sheets, pillows, and coverlets white as the driven snow." Advertisements stated "Nothing will be spared which will conduce to the comfort of guests." With the hotel's "homelike" meals and "genuine good coffee," it became the social center of the town.

The large white building in the center of Caribou was the Sherman House, one of the mining camp's early hotels. Author's collection.

Many of the men who called themselves miners in Boulder County at the time were unskilled laborers who had come west during the gold rush. Caribou mine owners recruited experienced hard-rock miners from Cornwall, England. They made their way across the Atlantic with their wives and children.

The "cousin Jacks," as they were called, came from a moderate climate near sea level and had to immediately adjust to long harsh winters at 10,000 feet. Many references were made to the climate in the "place where the winds are born." One miner is said to have exclaimed, "Gawd, I hope when summer does come, both days is nice!"

To get away from the bitter cold and wind, Abel Breed and O. B. Cutter, owners of the Caribou Lode, chose the town of Middle Boulder for the location of a mill to treat their silver ore. By this time, company representatives sailed to Holland (also called The Netherlands) and sold their properties to "The Mining Company Nederland of the Hague." Nederland was the Dutch word for Netherlands. In honor of the new company, Middle Boulder was renamed again and incorporated as Nederland.

The Caribou Mill, was, at the time, the largest silver processing mill in Colorado. The company's payroll was $14,000 per month. Eighteen men were employed in Nederland and one hundred men in the mine at Caribou. The ore was smelted into silver bullion and cast into bars which weighed approximately seventy pounds apiece. The bars were hauled by wagon to the First National Bank in Central City, then to the United States Mint in Denver.

Unfortunately, the company's management wasn't as farsighted as its dreams. A long list of unpaid miners filed a lien on the Caribou property. It was shut down in 1875, then purchased the next year at a tax sale by well-known Colorado investors Jerome B. Chaffee and David H. Moffat. The mine at Caribou and the mill at Nederland again went into production.

The first of three destructive fires roared into Caribou on September 14, 1879. Supposedly, the flames were started by careless campers on Arapaho Peak. Gale winds blew sparks into town. At the Caribou mine, the fire burned the shaft house and destroyed valuable machinery. Then the fire spread over the upper portion of town, jumped the Sherman House, and burned twenty-five dwellings in the lower section of town. A total of forty to sixty houses and mine buildings were leveled by the blaze.

By a stroke of luck, the central area of the town was saved. People rushed to Nederland for safety. Miraculously, there was no loss of life from the fire, but many of the miners had recently lost children to scarlet fever and diphtheria and became so discouraged by the fire that they moved away.

In 1878, during the silver boom, author Helen Hunt Jackson became one of Nederland's first tourists. She traveled by horseback from Central City to Boulder via Nederland. All along the way Jackson raved about the scenery but didn't think much of Nederland. She called it "a dismal little mining town, only a handful of small houses and smelting mills." Then she added, "Bowlder [Boulder] Creek comes dashing through it, foaming white to the very edge of the grimy street, reclaiming the land from dust and stones and making it soft and green for many an acre."

The main business district, at the time, consisted of just the one block of First Street west of Bridge Street. Buildings lined both sides of First Street. Bridge Street ran straight north and south, not curved as it is today.

Jackson wasn't impressed with the silver strikes in nearby Caribou, but other people were. By the time of the author's arrival, Nederland was a town of five hundred people. Mail arrived daily with stage lines to Caribou, Central City, and Boulder. Nederland even beat Boulder as the first town in Boulder County to have a telegraph office. Nederland was important to the outside world.

This early view of Nederland is looking south. The large building to the right of center is the Hetzer House Hotel. Author's collection.

As soon as silver was discovered in Caribou, Boulder road builders lost no time building a road up the previously-impassable and narrow Boulder Canyon. Caribou needed supplies, and Boulder wanted its business. With traffic still passing between Ward and Black Hawk, Nederland soon became a busy crossroads.

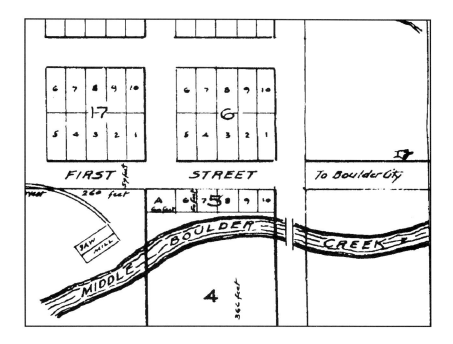

The town of Nederland was platted in 1877 with the business district centered on West First Street. Author's collection.

If you had arrived in town at the time and looked for a place to stay, you would have had a choice of accommodations. The Mountain House (also called the Middle Boulder House) stood alone on the northeast corner of Bridge and First Streets. An advertisement for the two-story frame hotel in the *Colorado Business Directory* stated, "Stages pass this House every day for Caribou, Central, Black Hawk, and Boulder. Good stables in connection with the House."

In 1872, J. W. Hetzer moved in from Black Hawk. After running the Mountain House for a couple of years, he built his own hotel, the Hetzer House, on the northwest corner of First and Jefferson Streets. According to the state directory, he claimed to have "the only first-class house in the place." A newspaper report called it "second to none in the hill country." Unlike the Mountain House a little over a block away, he said his was "Centrally located."

In this 1899 photo, the Mountain House is barely-visible on the right behind a tree. The Hetzer House is the white prominent building left of center. The false-fronted white building on the northwest corner of Bridge and First Streets is the Hetzer Saloon. (Compare to the photograph on page 105.) Carnegie Branch Library for Local History, Boulder Historical Society collection.

The Hetzer House was on the northwest corner of First and Jefferson Streets. It later was enlarged as the MacKenzie Hotel which burned in 1939. Carnegie Branch Library for Local History, Boulder Historical Society collection.

A third hotel in the early days was the Nederland House, "the most pleasantly-located house in town." It was located north of downtown near the school, and became the new stopping place for the four and six-horse Concord stagecoaches on their way between Boulder and Caribou. The hotel was run by Reverend James Connoran who also taught a well-attended Sunday school and led a young men's debating society.

One of the earliest commercial buildings on the north side of West First Street was a hardware store built by John H. Pickel in 1872. He carried drill steel, picks, shovels, hammers, blasting equipment, and other mining supplies. The building changed hands several times, and was later purchased by Colin McKenzie, who sold clothing, groceries, and provisions.

McKenzie was known as a "character." One day he fell down an outside stairway. Someone ran over, helped him up, and asked if he was hurt. He was said to have replied, "No, I always come down that way when I'm in a hurry."

In the 1880s, as the price of silver declined, Nederland's population fell correspondingly. Soon the Caribou silver mill lay idle most of the time. By 1892, when the town's population was only one hundred, Wesley Hetzer had taken over the Hetzer Hotel from his father. No other hotels were open at the time.

On December 26, 1899, Caribou suffered its second major fire. It started in Richie's general store, then burned all of the north side of Idaho Street. Peter Werley's building was one of first to go, and Caribou's first hotel, the Planter's House, was destroyed.

The rest of Caribou was granted a reprieve of a few more years. The Sherman House was still-standing although the locals called it the Uncle Billy Donald Hotel after new owner William Donald who ran it in the 1890s. Donald had been foreman of the Caribou mine, superintendent of the Native Silver and Seven Thirty mines, and manager of the Spencer mine. He seemed, however, to prefer the hotel business.

Another hotel was the Trollope House which became a social center, especially on Sunday afternoons. According to an interview with the late Eugene R. Trollope, he moved with his parents to Caribou in 1902. They leased a building up the street from the Sherman House and converted it to a "hotel and eating establishment." The Trollopes housed as many as thirty men year around for thirty dollars per month including room and board. Supposedly they were all retired miners who just lived there. They had seen the camp in its productive days and weren't about to leave.

In 1904, when the southern branch of the narrow gauge railroad was extended to Eldora, the trains stopped a few miles down the road at Cardinal, but were too late to help with the major output of the mines.

Caribou's third big fire, on November 14, 1905, burned both the Trollope House and the Sherman House, as well as a store and a meat market. By then, only the stubborn remained. A newspaper account stated, "Fire mercifully ended the prolonged agony of abandonment."

Yet a few hardy souls still made Caribou their home.

The Caribou Post Office stayed open until March, 1917, and was one of the town's last buildings. Courtesy Earl and Barbara Bolton.

The driver of this freight wagon posed for a photo just below Caribou, in 1899, the year of the mining camp's second major fire. The photograph is captioned "Caribou or Bust."
Courtesy Elmer Holmes.

NEDERLAND AND THE GOLD IN ELDORA

Gold discoveries in the early 1890s, in Cripple Creek west of Colorado Springs, stimulated renewed interest in gold prospecting throughout Colorado. Just a few miles upstream from Nederland, John Kemp panned Middle Boulder Creek and found small quantities of gold. He staked a placer claim and called it Happy Valley. A few more prospectors arrived and located additional claims in what first became known as Happy Valley Camp.

The first of many newspaper articles on the "new mining camp" appeared December 28, 1892, in the Central City *Register Call*. Glowing descriptions were given of each mining claim. The *Boulder Tribune* was more realistic and stated, "To the casual observer, the term Camp might seem ambitious, as at present it consists of two log cabins and a population of ten."

Soon more prospectors moved in and staked claims all over the mountainsides surrounding Happy Valley. Promising mines included the Enterprise and the Clara, as well as the Village Belle, Virginia, Terror, Bonanza, Gold Coin, and Bird's Nest.

Some were legitimate and some were not. Novices were duped when unscrupulous sellers salted their claims. One mine operator sold a placer claim by taking the buyers with him as he panned for gold. To show his "plentiful" gold, he panned in various locations. Before each spot he fumbled in his pocket for a fresh chew of tobacco. Besides the tobacco, his wet hands also picked up a liberal supply of gold dust easily transferred to the gravel being panned.

Happy Valley was renamed Eldorado by the time the post office was established on February 13, 1897. Mrs. Lois Holzhauser became the first postmistress. Right away she had a problem. Mail repeatedly ended up in Eldorado, California, so the town's name was shortened to Eldora.

Although silver had been just the first of three metals which influenced the growth of Nederland, the town welcomed Eldora's gold strikes, as it brought the prospectors, miners, investors, and the curious all over again.

In October, 1897, Agent Rodda of the Colorado Telephone Company commented, "Nederland, once a busy milling camp, seems to wear a look of inactivity at present [yet] the surrounding country near Nederland is very picturesque, and at this time of year it certainly presents a scene which would be hard to duplicate, even in scenic Colorado."

A few years before, Mary Roose and her husband moved from Boulder to Nederland to operate a ranch on Barker Meadows, since covered by Barker Reservoir. The family took in some boarders, then found themselves so busy they turned people away. Some, like Rodda, had discovered the scenery, but others were gold seekers on the way to Eldora.

Recently-widowed, in 1896, Mary Roose built a two-story hotel and named it the Antlers after the famous Antlers Hotel in Colorado Springs. Nederland's Antlers was built as a home and hotel combined. The Roose family's living quarters shared the first floor with the kitchen, dining room, and office. Fourteen guest rooms, numbered one through fifteen so no one would have the unlucky number thirteen, were on second floor.

Rates were five to ten dollars per week, or one to two dollars per night. Sons Frank and Oscar hauled groceries on their stage line up the single lane road through Boulder Canyon. A large stable accommodated up to twelve horses.

The Antlers Hotel was built on a hillside and commanded a great view of Barker Meadows, which became Lake Nederland after the building of the dam. The lake is now called Barker Reservoir.

The parlor of the Antlers Hotel was comfortable and refined.
Carnegie Branch Library for Local History,
Boulder Historical Society collection.

Above, the Antlers Hotel. Guests enjoyed the large open porch. Below, the hotel's dining room. Both photographs, Carnegie Branch Library for Local History, Boulder Historical Society collection.

ELDORA'S GOLD RUSH

Gold mining was intense in Eldora while it lasted. A number of mines on Spencer Mountain were individually worked from the surface. It soon became evident that a tunnel driven into the mountain would prove a more efficient way to haul out ore as well as drain the ever-accumulating water. Manager John A. Gilfillan organized the Mogul Drainage and Transportation Tunnel & Mining and Milling Company in July, 1897. Capital stock of one million shares was issued at one dollar per share.

The portal of the Mogul Tunnel was (and still is) near the base of Spencer Mountain opposite the center of town. Miners had only a short walk to work. The first sixty feet of the tunnel was painstakingly drilled by hand. Then a steam-powered power plant was installed with an air compressor which ran five machine drills and also ventilated the mine. Each shift extended the tunnel another four and one-half feet. After two years of intermittent labor, the Mogul Tunnel's eight-foot high by ten-foot wide double-track bore reached 830 feet under Spencer Mountain and intersected twenty-eight ore-bearing veins.

As soon as a new ore vein was crossed, a crew of men began drifting, or following the vein underground. The first gold mines to be worked through the tunnel were the Somerset, Grover Cleveland, and the Little Stranger. The individual mine owners gave the tunnel company a part interest in their mines as well as royalties on their production.

The gold ore was very rich in occasional "pockets," but, there weren't enough of them to be profitable. Treatment costs were high, and sales of the low-grade gold ore failed to pay production expenses. Somehow, Gilfillan managed, for a few years, to keep his miners employed. Making matters worse, the large Enterprise mill did not successfully process the ore. When mill Manager Neil Bailey missed a payday, his employees set his house on fire and shot him in the arm as he tried to put out the blaze. Bailey died a few days later.

At the height of its mining activity, Eldora boasted close to thirteen hundred inhabitants. Six to eight stagecoaches per day left fully-loaded from Boulder for the ride up Boulder Canyon. The steep narrow road, built for the silver strikes in Caribou, was one-way, with turnouts, and had numerous bridges. The coaches stopped at the Eureka House at "the narrows" where the driver changed horses, and he and his passengers ate a noon meal.

"Crowds continue to pour into this place," wrote a reporter. "The stages brought up over fifty passengers last Tuesday. Buildings are going up on all sides and everybody looks pleasant and very busy. The snow is bad in many portions of the district, but this doesn't stop business. A one-half interest in a property sold last week for eight hundred dollars. The nearest point the purchaser got to the property was about 3,900 feet. He examined its possibilities through a field glass."

All new arrivals needed a place to stay. "Sleeping apartments" were said to have been at a premium. A *Denver Republican* reporter stated, "The surveyors have not yet completed the survey of the Eldora townsite, and yet the sale of lots is continuous. Purchasers examine the plat and go out and guess at the probable location. This is not easy. The sawmills now in operation cannot supply one-half the lumber demanded, and a new mill is now on the ground, in process of erection, while two others are on the road." It was said that five or six new houses were started every day, and that the number would increase as the weather improved and more lumber was available.

By this time, Eldora had a variety of businesses including five saloons, a newspaper, a bank, a photograph gallery, two ladies' clubs, and a Methodist Church. The public school had two teachers and about ninety pupils. The first hotel was a small false-fronted frame building called the Vendome. The biggest saloon was Higgins and Foster which doubled as a gambling hall offering roulette, poker, and faro. Across the stream and separate from the town itself was Eldora's red light district, called Monte Carlo.

Only so much gold could be removed from underneath the ground, but carpenters could be kept busy indefinitely. A town full of substantial buildings might attract investors who could discover more gold. For a year or two, the theory worked well, but eventually mining in Eldora degenerated into a campaign to sell town lots. The Mayham Investment Company advertised, "We have about 600 lots for sale at from $50 to $100 per lot. We believe many of these hundred dollar lots will re-sell within 30 days for $1,000. To you who have made money in Cripple Creek, Leadville, Aspen, Creede, or any of the good camps of the State, here is your next opportunity. If you want one or more of these lots you should call at once, as the rate they are now selling there will be none left next Saturday."

Above, the Vendome (on the left) was built in 1896 and was Eldora's first hotel. Author's collection. *Below, this photograph taken the same year shows some of Eldora's earliest buildings. The Vendome is on the far right.* Courtesy Earl and Barbara Bolton.

An eloquent and optimistic newspaper reporter wrote, "The era of uncertainty and exploration in the district has passed, and the day of facts and development and production, and the steam whistle and rumble of ore wagons and thunder of machinery has dawned. The patient, persevering, weather-stained and horny-handed prospector is nearing the turn of the trail. The cabin is fading away in the mists, and out there is a home of luxury. It belongs to the mine manager or millionaire that is to be. In Eldora now it is only a matter of who it will be. The name of Eldora's mines are legion, and the treasures they contain passes human comprehension."

"West Eldora" during its building boom, ca. 1897. Author's collection.

Cut trees decorated Eldorado Avenue as a band played on Labor Day, 1899. This view is looking east. (Compare to photograph on page 106.) Courtesy Earl and Barbara Bolton.

THE GOLD MINER HOTEL

At the height of the real estate frenzy, every man in camp who could handle a saw or hammer was kept in constant employment. Even young boys got a dollar a night for holding lanterns for carpenters so they could see to drive nails.

It's no wonder, then, that the Randall brothers, I. J. and Jas. M., saw an opportunity in the hotel business and decided to build the two-story Gold Miner Hotel. At least one of the Randall brothers owned a sawmill. They took in as a third partner Alice A. Smith, wife of a Boulder real estate agent. In December, 1897, the three bought the lot on which the hotel now stands for fifty dollars. When Eldora was platted, the lot on the corner of 6th Street and Klondyke Avenue was called the "Smith-Randall" property.

The logs for the two and one-half story hotel were milled on all four sides, then carefully dove-tailed together by a skilled carpenter. According to Carolyn Olsen Hale's account of the Olsen family in the February, 1998, Eldora Civic Association newsletter, her grandfather, Olaf J. Olsen, a Norwegian carpenter, participated in the building of the hotel. No doubt he was responsible for the hand-crafted joints that have withstood a century of time.

In February, 1898, the *Denver Republican* stated that the "Randall Brothers and their associates have a 30-room hotel nearly completed." In order to have a more refined appearance toward the street, the entire front of the building was covered with clapboard siding and painted white.

Women, children, dogs, burros, and a few men turned out on this snowy day in front of the Gold Miner Hotel in 1899. Courtesy Elmer Holmes.

Mrs. Mena Given was the first manager of the Gold Miner Hotel. A *Denver Times* reporter praised her as "a little woman of German descent, with bright brown eyes and a soft low voice with which particularly womanly attractions she unites a determination of purpose which has made her noted all over Colorado." He continued, "Her only fault, her friends think, is her great tender-heartedness about bills. She is always overlooking some indebtedness and helping on some struggling fellow creature."

For twenty years, Mena Given had managed the Colorado

House, on the northwest corner of 13th and Pearl Streets, in Boulder. For a few years she managed the Albert Restaurant in Denver. She was said to have developed quite a following. Another reporter wrote,

"Eldora has become a great resort for people from Denver who feel that in going to Mrs. Given they are sure of being well-cared for. During the Biennial Federation of Clubs, which has just closed in Denver, a special invitation was given by Mrs. Given to the women to go up to Eldora and spend the night. Thus, an opportunity was offered to see the wonderful mining region in the heart of the mountains and a part of the work that a brave spirited woman has carried on in far-off mining camps."

Despite her obvious skill as a hostess, Given was described by former resident Donald Kemp as "rather aloof in manner." Even then it had been rumored that she had been the wife of Charles J. Giteau, who assassinated President James A. Garfield in 1881. Years later the rumor was proven not to be true. The real widow was a Mrs. Giben, who had been in the restaurant business in Chicago. Their similar names and occupations had caused the confusion.

The Eldora townsfolk retained their optimism. The Gold Miner Hotel often hosted receptions of the "Sunshine Society" where "The usual Sunshine hop was indulged in while those not disposed to dance were entertained at cards and games." The group joined together to sing a song entitled "God Bless the Sunshine" which began "Long may the cheering rays beam over Eldora and cheer the days of her people." At other times guests entertained each other. Some played mandolins while others sang solos. One woman was said to have "delighted the audience with some very clever slight of hand performances."

Evelyn (Mrs. John) Lilly and her son Harold Lilly are seated on the porch of the Gold Miner Hotel in this 1899 photo. Harold Lilly was the father of Eldora resident Barbara Bolton. Courtesy Earl and Barbara Bolton.

After the first town election, in May, 1898, the trustees granted a saloon license to the Gold Miner Hotel, the first establishment in Eldora to receive one. A month later, the hotel, still managed by Given, was sold to Charles W. Caryl of Denver for two thousand five hundred dollars.

Using funds of one hundred thirty thousand dollars, which he borrowed from an elderly lady, Caryl invested in mining properties, mostly in the town of Wall Street, in Four Mile Canyon. But he had other interests as well. Caryl invented a patent medicine called Vril, supposedly a cure-all "which could destroy the strongest army." As Chief of the Brotherhood of Light cult, he laid out a utopian community for Wall Street, but it was never completed.

In 1899, Caryl was sued by his investor. He then countersued which threw his assets into litigation. One of his listed assets was the Gold Miner Hotel. A participant in the lawsuit stated, "I only wish that there was something of value in the properties mortgaged to this lady that she might perchance secure some of her money back." Caryl had paid a high price for the Gold Miner Hotel, but less than two years after the height of the booms, property values collapsed. The hotel had already lost over half of its value and was assessed at one thousand dollars, with the lot at forty dollars. By 1901, the property decreased even more.

Caryl was stuck with the hotel, so he signed another lease with Given. In 1904, she moved away and Mrs. Louise Jamieson briefly took over the hotel's management before running the Hetzer House in Nederland.

Photographer Joseph Sturtevant ("Rocky Mountain Joe"), second from right, labeled this photo "Joe flips a flapjack at the Old Fourth of July Mine." The mine, west of Eldora on the road to Arapaho Pass, was last worked in 1904. This photo was taken prior to Sturtevant's death in 1910. Author's collection.

ELDORA AFTER THE BOOM

Six years passed between the height of Eldora's mining and real estate activities and the arrival of the railroad. When the trains did arrive the prospecting crowds had gone. The Monte Carlo girls left as soon as the easy money was over. In 1901, fires burned on seven nearby mountains, but fortunately the town was spared.

Mining in the Eldora area had not proved profitable. The biggest failure was the Fourth of July mine, high on the trail to Arapaho Pass. Years before, a tunnel had been dug to intersect a two-hundred foot shaft. Near the tunnel's portal were built a blacksmith shop, a steam power plant, a two-story boarding house, manager's quarters, bunkhouses, stables, and storage sheds.

The mine had been idle for many years when, in 1904, promoters decided it should be reworked. English-born Amos Entwistle was the mine foreman. The ore was said to be rich in copper. Three million shares of stock, at one dollar per share, were quickly purchased by eastern investors. A decision was made to add another tunnel.

Inexperienced men backed by greed, rather than mining engineers, were involved in the boring of the tunnel. Suspense ran high as the crew blasted the rock and hauled away the debris. Investors followed the miners' every move in order to be the first to see the great wealth believed to be hidden inside the mountain.

Just when the miners expected to enjoy the fruits of their labor, they stared in horror and disbelief. Instead of seeing ore they saw daylight. They had bored a semicircular tunnel and came out only a few feet from where they had begun. The Fourth of July mine never reopened again.

Besides Entwistle, a few other residents remained from Eldora's boom days. John A. Gilfillan continued as manager of the Mogul Tunnel. By 1904, he had overseen the completion of six thousand feet of underground workings. The editor of the *Eldora Record* wrote, "[Gilfillan's] services are in great demand from mine owners and investors. When he passes on a property the investor can rest assured his report will be correct, as the writer believes Mr. Gilfillan can see into a rock just a little farther than the average mining engineer."

Robert H. B. Little and wife Minnie were a young couple from Illinois when they arrived in Eldora in 1898. Little ended up serving two terms as mayor. He also managed three mines but none were profitable. His last investment was the Revenge mine above Lost Lake. The mine often flooded with water, and the ore was mostly low-grade. In 1907 the Littles gave up and left Eldora.

The number of businesses had sharply decreased since the boom days. In 1904, A. F. Sisson ran the only saloon left in town. The Vendome Hotel had closed its doors, but the Gold Miner Hotel and another called the Eldora Hotel continued to accommodate travelers. The only other businesses included a blacksmith shop, the telephone company, a confectionery, a drug store, a hardware store, a livery stable, a meat market, a restaurant, a shoe shop, the *Eldora Record* newspaper, and Mills & La Point's Groceries.

Charles LaPoint and his wife Ann were from Iowa. They had arrived prior to 1898. Charles quickly gave up prospecting and mining for a half interest in a general store. His partner, N. M. Mills, was called "Fatty." In their book, Kemp and Langley wrote, "He reminded one of a monstrous [nursery rhyme character] Humpty-Dumpty. In the tradition of fat men, he seemed to be ever in a jovial humor, and from morn till night was never without his pipe, usually a corncob."

This man, who was said to have resembled Humpty Dumpty, is presumed to be N. M. "Fatty" Mills. Courtesy Earl and Barbara Bolton.

Mills's vest was threadbare down the front. His shirtsleeves were frayed at the elbows from continuous leaning against the counter at the store as well as constant friction with the edge of a card table. When business was slow, he could always be found in one of the saloons with cards in one hand and pipe in the other.

Another old-timer was Iowa-born B. J. Hardin. His mother had died when he was a baby. He then became orphaned at the age of two when his father drowned during the California gold rush. Hardin fought and was wounded in the Civil War, then went to college and taught school in Illinois. In Eldora he invested in the Village Belle and other mines, and put his money into commercial buildings. He also purchased the waterfalls above Hessie and intended to build a power plant. According to a report in a 1904 *Eldora Record,* "Some kind of a political hoodoo has been his Nemesis ever since his election as justice of the peace." Hardin married Eliza McLauchland, a much younger woman, born "at sea" in 1882. Their son Charles, a bookkeeper, also became a justice of the peace. The Hardins stayed at least through 1916.

Most of Eldora's remaining residents were bachelors who had come during the Eldora gold rush and had no other place to go. The men looked out for each other. If they needed something they borrowed it, and they could always charge groceries at the store. Reversing the trend was Mogul Tunnel manager John Gilfillan. He finally got discouraged, left Eldora, married, and farmed near Platteville.

A few of the residents, however, were women. By 1904, twenty-eight called Eldora their home. Five women were either widowed or divorced. Twenty-three others quietly assumed their roles as housewives, except for "Missouri Ann." According to Kemp and Langley she was nearly six feet tall, powerfully-built, and plain-featured. She smoked, chewed, swore, fought, and drank while cutting and hauling logs to a sawmill. Her husband accompanied her, but meekly stayed in the background.

Missouri Ann also worked as a cook's helper for various mining companies. One time she attacked the female cook with a meat saw. It was said that the woman's steel corset saved her life as Ann had her pinned to a table and was attempting to saw her in two.

In 1916, the long-abandoned Enterprise mill was torn down and the lumber sold for salvage. Eldora's early mining days were over.

Eldora was the southern terminus of the narrow gauge railroad known as the Switzerland Trail of America. The trains reached the town after the major mining activities were over. Author's collection.

TOURISTS DISCOVER ELDORA

Colorado & Northwestern Railroad's President Samuel B. Dick envisioned his narrow gauge line connecting with the Denver, Northwestern & Pacific (Moffat Road) then being built on Rollins Pass over the Continental Divide into Middle Park. The logical route for the Colorado & Northwestern, also called "The Switzerland Trail" would be south from Sunset and through Eldora. Dick firmly believed that the railroad's arrival in Eldora would revitalize the production from the Mogul Tunnel, but it didn't.

Shortly after Christmas, in 1904, the end of the line was a point six thousand feet below Eldora. From there, the first train delivered one hundred or so dignitaries who walked the rest of the way. At the Gold Miner Hotel they were served a turkey dinner. Regular rail service began in January, 1905, but heavy snow plagued the line for months to come.

Finally a small depot was completed near the center of town. The two-room building sheltered people on one side and baggage on the other. A tiny office and telegraph room were squeezed in-between. Arrival time for the express train, which carried passengers and mail, was just after noon every day. Everyone not otherwise occupied went to the depot to meet the train.

Ben Hilliard O'Connor, born in Eldora in 1901, once

described the scene,

"As the last mile or so was uphill, the little engine chugged along at a fair clip until it reached the exact spot when its own momentum would propel it to the unloading platform where it would stop of its own accord. While Mr. Reed, who was the conductor, guide, and public relations agent, informed the passengers about food, departure, time, and so on, the brakeman set enough brakes to hold the train. Just as the train came into sight every day, Mr. Lilly, who ran the Livery Stables, would harness his team to the spring wagon which carried passengers to Lake Eldora, and, later in the afternoon, trunks and other impediments to the various cottages. How he could harness his team and arrive at the station at exactly the same time as the train, I have never understood. But he always did, clattering across the bridge over the creek and circling the public scale with a crack of the whip and a throaty 'haw' as the team came to a stop at precisely the same spot every day."

Col. David Barrett was a night "hostler" in Eldora during the summers of 1911 and 1912. After the freight train arrived late in the afternoon, his job was to shake down the fire in the locomotive, fish out the coal clinkers, clean out the ashes, sweep out the coach, and wash the windows. He then had to bank the fire in the locomotive and spend the night adding to the fire and watching the steam gauge to see that the boiler pressure didn't get too low to get up steam the next morning.

When interviewed in the 1940s, Barrett said one of the sights he never forgot was "watching the Shay engine toiling up the gentle grade into Eldora, hissing like a huge teakettle and spewing steam from a number of joints." He added that the Shay, a slow-geared engine, was only used as a last resort when all the other engines were on regular runs or pulling excursions to Glacier Lake.

Despite the dreams of its officials, the railroad couldn't revitalize Eldora's gold production. The estimated tonnage just wasn't there. Plans to cross the Divide were abandoned. Ward was the terminus of the northern branch of the line and Eldora was the end of the line to the south.

That was just fine with the tourists who had enjoyed railroad excursions to Ward and were ready for a change of scenery. The railroad company moved its huge picnic pavilion from Mont Alto (between Sunset and Ward) to Glacier Lake so Eldora-bound passengers could add rowing to their leisure activities.

The first excursion to Eldora ran on April 30, 1905, and was followed by "wild flower specials." These trains would stop at various places along the way and allow everyone time to get off and gather large bouquets.

"No one who has not taken the trip to Eldora this summer has any conception of the varied beauties displayed by nature in the wealth of wild flowers which the hillsides display," wrote a *Daily Camera* reporter. "Columbines, lilies, roses, mountain honeysuckle are all now in the fresh glory of their beauty and the mountains for long distances are fairly carpeted with blue and pink and red — all the colors of the rainbow. We speak of these things after a two days sojourn along the 'Switzerland Trail.' To miss the sight is to lose something freshening and inspiring for never in our experience of thirty-one years of Boulder County summers have we seen Nature so bountiful with her floral gifts."

University of Colorado summer school students also arrived

in Eldora on the train for weekly climbs up South Arapaho Peak. The first day of the organized camping trip involved walking from Eldora to a base camp near today's Fourth of July campground. The next day the groups passed the shaft house of the abandoned Fourth of July mine and scaled the 13,397-foot peak. Skilled climbers, who had gone on ahead, greeted them at the top with prepared lunches. The students crawled into their bedrolls again at base camp before their hike back to the waiting train in Eldora.

The same year the railroad arrived in Eldora, Mrs. Sarah Martin became the manager of the Gold Miner Hotel. The Iowa native had been in town since 1898. Kemp and Langley described her as follows,

" 'Ma' was rather plump in build, and decidedly sharp of tongue, especially toward those whom she disliked. Tourists were a sore trial to 'Ma,' even though she was largely dependent on their patronage for a living. When her ire was roused by some hapless newcomer she was prone to erupt with a verbal volley, which, though picturesque, would not always pass the censor. On one occasion a group had gotten in bad and 'Ma' was 'on the prod.' Snorted she, 'Some more of God's mistakes; comin' in camp with a dirty shirt an' a dollar bill; and they won't change either all the time they're here!' "

In the early 1890s, Sarah's husband James Martin had run the Belvidere House, a hotel and boarding house on the southwest corner of Walnut and 12th Street (now Broadway), in Boulder. It was there that Sarah filed for divorce stating that James "cruelly misused" her. She ran the hotel herself before she moved to Eldora. Despite being outspoken, Sarah was well-liked by her neighbors. "Mrs. Martin is always looking for the opportunity to make things pleasant for the home people and for the stranger within the gates," wrote a reporter for the *Eldora Record*. "If there is an entertainment to be given, or a dance to be held, it is always Mrs. Martin who is looked to as the organizer. Mrs. Martin has three sons, who are well liked and who are a credit to any community. The oldest two, Harry and Fred, are miners, and are considered by all who have employed them as very capable and steady workers."

The only person in town at the time with a telephone was Harry Martin. He ran for mayor on the anti-saloon ticket. Those who wanted to call him simply asked the operator for "Silver 33."

"Mrs. Martin makes her hotel home-like and cheerful for her guests and her table is the best in the mountain hotels," added the reporter. "Traveling men and visiting tourists and mining men will find this the place to stay when they come to Eldora. Mrs. Martin is also interested in several mining claims in the camp which bid fair to become valuable properties with development. Her youngest son, Homer, is a schoolboy, and is well liked by his comrades. We have employed him in the *Record* office on several occasions and have always found him a willing and faithful worker."

The Gold Miner Hotel was advertised as a headquarters for commercial and mining men, but it also extended an invitation to tourists. Its advertisements stated, "Summer tourists are invited to spend their vacation at this beautiful health-giving resort. The best the market has will be provided at this hotel. Come spend the summer months here." Hotel rates were two dollars per day.

In 1910, newspapers covered the death of the Gold Miner

Hotel's first manager, Mena Given. She died at the Kiowa Lodge in Bailey, Colorado. Given was remembered as "a hard-working woman who gave much to charity and never turned a hungry man away from her restaurants."

Although Sarah Martin was considered an efficient businesswoman, the Gold Miner Hotel went into foreclosure, then was redeemed by its owner, Caryl, for twenty-four dollars. In 1912, Caryl was jailed for sending "obscene matter" (possibly birth control information) through the mails after attempting to "work out the problem of a higher civilization through the perfection of the sexes." In 1915, this man with the grandiose plans sold the hotel to Alice Ross for a ten dollar gold coin.

The mining industry had failed and property was practically worthless, but the scenery remained the same. Tourism was actively promoted. A reporter for a Greeley newspaper wrote in the teens,

"There are no cottages for rent such as are known at Manitou, Estes Park, and other higher-priced resorts. The houses are cabins, pure and simple, former homes of the mining population of several years ago. They are of pine logs, or native lumber, lined with building paper, and have rain-tight roofs, are furnished plainly, primitive, but comfortable. There are no bedbugs. Two very good general stores carry practically everything needed for the table, and the Boulder gardens furnish plenty of fruit and vegetables that are shipped fresh daily to the stores. The two hotels of Eldora [Gold Miner Hotel and Eldora Hotel] furnish day board for $5 to $6 a week for those who do not want to cook or keep house. The price of furnished cabins runs from $4 for the very cheapest, to $10 a week for the largest and best, with an average of $6 or $7 for a good one of two or three rooms."

One writer who obviously got carried away described the town as "Eldora, the land of gold; place of scenic grandeur and numberless charms. It is one of the wonder places of the American continent. Perched up there among the clouds on the crest of the continent, it rivals the wildest scenes in the Alps or the marvelous landscapes in the Andes."

Meanwhile, the Colorado & Northwestern Railroad sold out to the Denver, Boulder & Western Railroad, nicknamed the "drink beer and wine" by its passengers. They still had fun, but the days of the railroad were numbered.

After the World War, tourists preferred the freedom of their newly-acquired automobiles. At the same time, the Denver Boulder & Western couldn't meet its expenses. When a flood, in 1919, washed out much of the track and many bridges, the railroad did not rebuild. It was the end of the line.

LAKE ELDORA RESORT

When Eldora guests and residents wanted a spectacular view of the mountains, they hiked to Peterson Lake on Spencer Mountain. Agent Rodda, the Colorado Telephone Company representative who was impressed with the scenery around Nederland, stopped there in 1897. He described it as "a pleasantly-situated lake about one and one-half miles from Eldora. He stayed overnight and stated, "The lake is well-filled with good-sized trout, which are, however, a little wary of the hook. Our host Peterson made us very comfortable overnight, and in the early morning we left for home [Central City]."

The writer of an 1899 newspaper supplement called *Lake Ha Ha Tonka* (another name for Peterson Lake) glowingly wrote,

"It lies from 8,000 to 11,000 feet above the sea. It is nearly two miles higher than the great agricultural areas and busy marts of the seaboard and the Mississippi valley, and a mile above the arid wastes of the desert. It looms far above the alfalfa fields and orchards of the intermountain valleys. It is a land of lovely lakes, of dancing brooks and purling streams and leaping cataracts. A realm of wild retreats, of dizzy heights and gaping gorges. Hills robed in eternal green, valleys bathed in sunshine, and the balmiest breezes that ever blew. It is more than this. It is the final realization of 'green fields far away.' It is the gold hunter's Mecca, where weary pilgrims may rest and worship at the shrine of the 'Blind Goddess' with a reason for the hope that is in them; with logic for the basis of their devotion."

Next to Peterson Lake was Lake Eldora. In 1904, Lake Eldora was purchased by the Eldora Resort and Power Company. By then the fish were biting and it was considered "a trout fisher's paradise." The company, which included Colorado Governor Alva Adams and Colorado & Northwestern Railroad officials, built a log dining hall called the Pine Log Lodge. They also added several rustic cabins and cottages and provided rowboats for the fishermen.

The Eldora Resort and Power Company had originally been formed to provide electricity and water to Eldora and the surrounding mines. In 1908, its members planned an aerial tramway intending to "capture some of the spare change of the many tourists who go over the Switzerland Trail every summer" by "hauling the passengers up in buckets." Neither the power plant nor the tramway ever materialized.

Pine Log Lodge was still popular in 1914. In August of that

year, the Boulder *Daily Camera* listed the names and addresses of over one hundred guests. About half were from Greeley, Colorado, while others came from the Midwest and California. A number were young families.

In addition, several other families stayed in private cottages. The late Isabel Hansen Cross and her family stayed in the Lake Eldora Inn, formerly the Pine Log Lodge, in 1917, the last year it was open. She described it as "a family and fishing resort with a pier on the lake, boats, and good fishing."

Another building at Lake Eldora was Dixie Lodge, complete with a Japanese-style bridge. Carnegie Branch Library for Local History, Boulder Historical Society collection.

According to the late Jack Langley, Denver socialite Annie

Morris built a vacation home, in 1914, complete with a Japanese-style bridge, and called it Dixie Lodge. Isabel Hansen Cross remembered looking across the lake from Lake Eldora Inn and seeing white-coated servants on the porch. Others in Eldora remember that on a clear night they could hear music from the resort. Eldora resident Barbara Bolton said that her mother, Edna Lilly, and her aunt, Glenn Phebus, played piano and violin for the guests.

After the mid-twenties, the Lake Eldora buildings sat vacant for many years. In 1992, Isabel Hansen Cross wrote, "For many summers, from the 1920s to the 1950s, visitors in Eldora Valley hiked the trail up Spencer Mountain to the lake to enjoy the scenery and explore the area. Some puzzled about the history of the large important-looking buildings and marveled that all was deserted."

"Lake Eldora Inn [the former Pine Log Lodge] burned to the ground in mid-winter 1964 or 1965," she continued. "Fortunately, it was surrounded by a large snowbank which kept the flames from spreading.... Behind the Inn there had been a pine building that served as a kitchen and dining room. It even had a huge restaurant-size wood-burning cookstove and a large square grand piano. This building did not burn with the Inn fire, but in later years just deteriorated and fell down."

"On a very dry and windy night in the fall of 1969, Dixie Lodge burned," she added. "Sparks from the fire were blown to Marysville. Only the huge chimney of the lodge remained."

TRAIN TO THE TOP OF THE WORLD

When prospectors first arrived in Boulder County, in 1858, Utes wintered on the plains. Every spring they headed home to Middle Park. Their route took them up Sunshine Canyon, down Poorman Hill to Four Mile Canyon, west to Sugar Loaf Mountain and through Gordon Gulch to Nederland. Then they continued on to Sulphide Flats, up to Lake Eldora, and from there up and over today's Rollins Pass.

Journalist Amos Bixby recounted one brief run-in between Boulder County gold prospectors and these native Americans. As the story goes, a man by the name of Barker was shot by a passing band of Utes in Gold Hill, in 1859. Twenty-nine volunteers mounted their horses and were said to have "chased the Indians over the range by way of South Boulder [Rollins] Pass."

New Hampshire-born John Quincy Adams Rollins had been farming in Illinois when gold was discovered in Colorado. Like many other men, he contracted "gold fever" and set off to seek his fortune. In a wagon train of thirty wagons, he arrived late in the summer of 1860 and set up a six-stamp gold mill in a community he called "Gold Dirt," now Rollinsville. He made over one thousand dollars the first week and was so encouraged that he enlarged his mill and staked and purchased many of the mining claims in the area.

He also made other investments. Rollins operated a "salt works" in South Park, an overland stage line with D. A. Butterfield, a hotel in Cheyenne, several roads in what now is Gilpin County, and the Rollins Pass wagon road over the Continental Divide.

Rollins was an entrepreneur who wasn't afraid to take risks. His late son, John Q. A. Rollins, Jr. claimed that the senior Rollins once made $11,000 playing billiards. The story is as follows —

"In 1866 Mr. Rollins turned up in Denver. The city was filled with men who won fortunes at various pursuits one day and lost them the next. About two o'clock in the afternoon, Mr. Rollins dropped into a billiard room over Brendlinger's cigar store, at the intersection of Blake and F Streets. The room was filled with amateurs and professionals. Among the former was Charles A. Cook, at that time a banker, and since then, strange to say, one of the wealthiest men in the Territory."

"Cook and Rollins entered into conversation. After exhausting the subjects of real estate and mining, the talk ran upon billiards. Cook appeared to have considerable confidence in his own skill, and laughed at Rollins when the latter said that he could beat him. This excited Rollins's indignation, and he finally asserted that he could give Cook twenty points in a hundred and lay him out. Cook said that he couldn't do it for four hundred dollars a game, and Rollins thought that he could. So a match was then and there arranged, playing to begin immediately."

The men took off their coats and began playing at three o'clock in the afternoon. They lit lamps and cigars and kept score with marks on the floor. Word of the match spread around the city and spectators crowded in to watch. As the evening wore on the money steadily oozed from Cook's pocket into that of Rollins.

"At midnight the spell was broken," continued his son. "Rollins showed signs of fatigue and Cook began to win. So elated was the latter that he proposed to raise the stakes from four hundred to eight hundred dollars a side. The room was packed, and scores of persons were glued together about the doors. Cook continued to win until an hour before daylight when Rollins got his second wind. The wheel of fortune began to run the other way. Cook's bad luck returned. He struggled like a man in the slough of despond, but it was of no use. The chalk marks ran up against him in spite of every effort."

All day long the game continued. Businesses were closed so their owners could watch the match. Rollins was ahead by noon, then Cook seemed to catch up and by evening fell behind again. After thirty-two hours, the players were said to have looked like ghosts. An hour before midnight, Rollins forfeited one thousand, but kept his winnings of eleven thousand dollars.

In the same spirit of adventure, Rollins unsuccessfully competed with Captain Edward L. Berthoud in a race to see who could be the first to complete a wagon road from the eastern side of the Continental Divide into Middle Park. Berthoud's Georgetown, Empire & Middle Park Wagon Road, now U. S. 40 over Berthoud Pass, eventually captured Middle Park's commerce and trade.

When Rollins worked on his road west of Gold Dirt (Rollinsville), he was fascinated by stone remains of "settlements or battlefields" on the nearly level summit. In an 1873 article in the *Rocky Mountain News* Rollins wrote,

"I have often wondered, as I have passed over the range, what had caused this singular formation — these rock pits and these long, regularly tall stone walls. Here are stone walls, two or three miles in length, compact and regular, apparently to mark the boundaries of lots and parcels of land."

"Nearby, and on either side of the walls, are numerous rock pits, round, and from one to four feet deep and from four to eight feet across the top, the whole exhibiting skill and workmanship that fully convinces me that this has been the work of human hands, and that these have probably been 'war pits.' Following the stone wall to the corners of the fields I found large flat rocks, eight feet across. These were laid on top, in line with the walls, as if to mark the true course of the different possessions. There were piled on tops of these rocks, in a line with one wall, stones from one to two feet high, leading directly to the corner of the fields. In this stone corner of the field I found a bow, about three feet in length, made from hemlock wood and having the appearance of great antiquity. The grain of the wood is worn from the bow fully a quarter of an inch deep, leaving knots protruding."

Some of the rocks may have been carried to the top of the pass by the Utes, as described by the late Wesley Hetzer on page 2. Remains of other rock formations can still be found. Recent archeologists, who have found similar rock walls on Arapaho and other Front Range passes, believe that the "war pits" described by Rollins actually were built for game drives. As herds of elk and big horn sheep followed their migration routes they were driven through the built-up rock area and then ambushed by hiding Indians.

The route Rollins followed at the time was called "the old

Ute trail." White settlers had managed to cross into Middle Park with a few wagons as early as 1862, but travel was extremely difficult. By 1873, Rollins had significantly improved his Rollinsville and Middle Park Wagon Road. He officially opened it by charging a toll.

Maintaining the road required considerable effort. In the summer of 1880, 14 year-old teamster Martin Parsons first crossed Rollins Pass with a group of men and twelve thousand head of Texas cattle. Of the section of the wagon road still visible above Yankee Doodle Lake he recorded, "The east side of this Pass had two steep hills which formed a V-shaped gulch between them. Every summer Mr. Rollins would build a cribbing of logs in this gulch and would fill the center with rocks and earth which helped reduce the grade between the hills."

Although Berthoud's route from Georgetown was preferred for wagon traffic, railroad builders took a close look at Rollins Pass. In 1880, they incorporated the Denver, Utah & Pacific Railway. The company built a still-visible grade above Eldorado Springs, but the railroad never materialized.

Then, in 1903, surveyors for the Denver, Northwestern & Pacific Railway looked at the wagon road again as a proposed route for a standard gauge railroad line. Even then, a tunnel through the Continental Divide was considered necessary. A "temporary" rail route over Rollins Pass was recommended as a way to work from both sides on a long and expensive tunnel.

The new railroad company completed their grade, laid track, and began running trains "over the hill" in 1904, the same year the "Switzerland Trail of America" pulled into Eldora.

As soon as it opened, the Denver, Northwestern & Pacific Railway was popular with Denver tourists and those who just wanted to escape the heat of the plains. The first stop, after Rollinsville, was Tolland. Special excursion trains called "picnic specials" took one thousand or more people to the small resort on a single day.

The original brick and tile Moffat depot in Denver had been torn down and was rebuilt brick by brick at Tolland. The small enclosed building had a large covered waiting area. A picnic and dance pavilion was built along with a hotel, lunch room, and several souvenir shops.

Tourists were lured with literature which promised them "The greatest short scenic trip in the world. New and elegant equipment, huge engines and vestibuled coaches combined with a perfect roadbed, make the trip one of exceptional enjoyment. Wild flowers grow luxuriantly among the mountains, and South Boulder Creek affords good fishing. Excellent lunches and hotel accommodations can be obtained at Tolland."

More adventurous tourists were urged to ride the train out of the mountain valley, up the "Giant's Ladder" of switchbacks, and on to the top of the pass. Corona, at 11,600 feet, was the highest standard gauge railroad station in North America. Tourist called it the "top of the world." The train ride from Denver to Corona was billed as a trip "from sultry heat to Colorado's north pole." Tourists picked wild flowers while standing on banks of perpetual snow.

The late author and historian Forest Crossen worked as a telegraph operator at Corona in the summer of 1926. He and two other co-workers provided the only link to the outside world. Crossen worked the graveyard shift and received a salary of fifty-eight cents per hour.

"Everything on the ride up there was new to me," he said.

"What impressed me the most were all the snowsheds full of smoke and gas. It was May 20, 1926, but the snow was packed up fourteen feet on the boxcars that served as our living quarters and telegraph office. The man I replaced was so anxious to go that he had his bags packed before he even trained me. We climbed in and out of the roof, the only place to walk."

Later in the summer when the snow finally did melt, Crossen took long walks or rode the train to Yankee Doodle Lake to fish. "It was kind of an outlaw railroad, a place of last resort for men who'd been fired from other railroad jobs," he said. "One man was an alcoholic who'd stolen money from the Santa Fe, and some of the others had been involved in wrecks. The place was so isolated that no one wanted to go there."

The following numbers correspond to the map on page 59.

#1. While still along the creek, look to the northwest to see the "Giant's Ladder," a series of switchbacks on the mountainside, necessary for the railroad to gain elevation without going over a four per cent grade.

#2. Tolland was the resort which catered to Denver tourists who sought quick relief from the heat of the plains.

#3. From here you can drive about one mile farther west to the east portal of the Moffat Tunnel. With luck, you might see one of the regularly-scheduled trains enter or exit the 6.21-mile tunnel to the Western Slope.

#4. The auto road bypasses a caved-in tunnel at this point, but if you walk up the old railroad grade, you'll come to a square water tower, one of the few ever built in the United States.

#5. Below here are the remains of Ladora, a town which housed section crews while the road was under construction in 1903 and 1904. Later it was home to loggers.

#6. The steep four per cent grade caused a Mallet engine to go off the tracks here and dump its load of coal down the mountainside.

#7. The railroad company cut down the trees along this stretch to build snowsheds and to prevent forest fires generated by flying cinders.

#8. Called Spruce wye, this was the turnaround point for the rotary snowplows that ran at least every eight hours during winter storms. A two-story building housed telegraph operators, section men, and snowplow crews.

#9. Yankee Doodle Lake was considered the most popular scenic spot on the railroad. The pile of rock extending into the lake came from the Denver Utah & Pacific Railway's attempts to bore a tunnel under the Continental Divide in 1880.

#10. Dixie Siding was the highest water stop on the east side of the summit. The railroad company named it Dixie at the request of a passenger from the South who wanted a balance with the northern name of Yankee Doodle.

#11. This tunnel on the skyline at the end of a straight stretch of road resembles a needle and its eye, so it was named Needle's Eye Tunnel.

#12. A section of Rollins's original wagon road runs just south of, but parallel to, the section of the railroad grade with the twin trestles.

#13. Named for the Spanish word for crown, Corona was the station at the top of Rollins Pass. After picking wild flowers, travelers enjoyed a meal in the railroad company's restaurant. Also at the station were employee housing and extensive snowsheds for as many as a dozen helper engines.

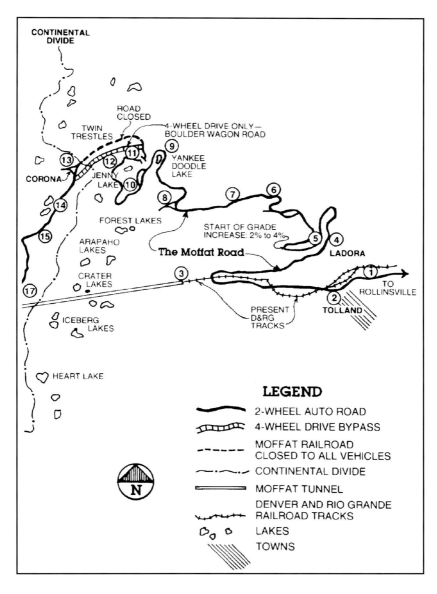

This map shows the east side of Rollins Pass.
Courtesy Rollins Pass Restoration Association.

Above, a jeep followed the railroad grade around Jenny Lake in 1954. The Needle's Eye Tunnel is visible in the background. Below, debris from the collapsed snowsheds often had to be cleared in order for drivers to continue on their way.
Both photos, author's collection.

In 1912, the Denver, Northwestern & Pacific Railway became the Denver & Salt Lake Railroad, more commonly called the "Moffat Road" after its late founder David Moffat. In 1913, a one-story brick hotel, with extensive eaves, was built to the north of the Corona station. Because of the fierce winds on the summit, cables secured the roof to the surrounding bedrock.

The "temporary route" over the pass was finally discontinued when the Moffat Tunnel opened in 1927. The average running time for passenger trains from dropped from two and one-half hours (in good weather) to only twelve minutes. Soon passengers on the Denver & Rio Grande Western's Panoramic and Exposition Flyer trains whizzed through the tunnel, oblivious of the spectacular scenery they missed.

Tourists had no way to get to Corona, but they still relaxed and picnicked in Tolland. One morning, in September, 1934, a passing engine threw off sparks which landed on top of the restaurant. The roof erupted into flames, then the building burned to the ground.

Beginning in 1935, tracks, ties, and some of the trestles were removed from the abandoned "hill route." The hotel at Corona was torn down. From then until 1956 the old railroad grade was utilized by a new breed of tourists, the four-wheel drive enthusiasts. These adventurers managed to drive between Rollinsville and Winter Park, although they often had to remove fallen timbers from snowsheds in order to continue on their way.

In 1956, the Colorado Division of Wildlife joined Boulder, Gilpin, and Grand Counties in improving the Rollins Pass road. Culverts were installed and the road surfaced with gravel. So that automobiles could follow the route, sturdy bridge timbers were laid over the Devil's Slide Trestles after the rails had been removed. Snowplows opened the road by July 4th of each year. The route remained open until the heavy snows came in the fall.

In 1979, the Rio Grande Zephyr stopped at Tolland for a seventy-fifth celebration of the resort's opening. Officials on the special train stayed for a brief program, then continued to Glenwood Springs and points west. Commemorative activities continued throughout the day.

Former resident and retired postal inspector Robert B. Clifton came from California to participate. In the town's early days his mother had run the post office while his father and a partner operated Tolland's general store.

Also in 1979, falling rocks closed the west portal of the Needle's Eye Tunnel. Rock bolts and wire mesh were installed in an attempt to stabilize the walls of the tunnel before it was reopened to auto traffic in September, 1987. It was closed again by a second rockfall in July, 1990. Currently the road is blocked above Forest Lakes, within walking distance of the Needles Eye tunnel and the summit.

Although the entire railroad grade was listed on the National Register of Historic Places, in 1980, an amendment and boundary increase, in 1997, added sections of the original Rollinsville and Middle Park Wagon Road. Specifically these included the cribbed road above Yankee Doodle Lake and the section between the Needles Eye Tunnel and Corona. Both have retained their historic integrity and were deemed worthy of inclusion in the historic district.

MAGNOLIA AND UPPER BOULDER CANYON

The Utes may have been the first people to cross Rollins Pass, but they didn't all go via Peterson Lake and Lake Eldora. Some of the Indians branched off on a new trail over the ridge above Magnolia, headed for Black Hawk instead of Middle Park. They rode their horses up the east side of Sugarloaf Mountain, then down through Switzerland Park to Boulder Canyon, and then uphill again to the old Hetzer ranch southwest of the townsite of Magnolia. The Utes chose the ranch location so their horses could graze in fields of high grass. At least a hundred arrow and spear heads have been found at their campsite.

During the early days of the Colorado gold rush, the most heavily-traveled route from the plains to Black Hawk and the mines near Central City was the Enterprise Road from Golden thru Golden Gate Canyon. Boulder investors decided to direct the traffic their way and formed the Boulder Valley and Central City Wagon Road Company to connect with the Enterprise Road. Construction began in March, 1865.

This new road followed Boulder Canyon to the foot of Magnolia Hill. The road then followed the route of the Utes up and over Magnolia Hill, across South Boulder Creek near the mouth of Beaver Creek (west of Pine Cliff), and then joined with the Enterprise Road to continue on to Black Hawk. Burro trains headed to Nathaniel Hill's smelter climbed the steep Magnolia mountainside loaded with sacks of ore from Boulder County mines.

This photograph of the the mining camp of Magnolia was taken by Joseph Sturtevant before 1910. Author's collection.

In 1875, prospectors discovered rich gold deposits in the Sac and Fox, Keystone, and Mountain Lion mines. The town of Magnolia was settled near the mines about two miles above Boulder Canyon. Boarding houses were built for miners, but Magnolia never became a tourist destination. Lee and Walter Smith operated a daily stage line from Boulder. Their coaches were specially designed for mountain roads and were drawn by mules instead of horses.

Instead of tourism, the mining camp of Magnolia became connected with a nineteenth-century celebrity. In 1890, at the age of 25, Elizabeth Cochrane was an investigative reporter for the *New York World.* She used the pen name of "Nellie Bly," taken from a popular Stephen Foster song. Bly explored many social issues, even feigning mental illness in order to get into and write about an insane asylum.

Meanwhile, Jules Verne's book, *Around the World in Eighty Days,* caught the imagination of the American people. Bly's editors liked her work and wanted to build their newspaper's circulation. They sent Bly around the world to try to outdo the book's main character, Phileas Fogg. Bly cabled on-the-scene stories to her newspaper which traced her progress and publicized every segment of her journey.

The slight five-foot-three brunette's trip lasted seventy-two days, so the public had a lot to read. Bly became an instant national celebrity when she arrived back in New York. Clothes, games, and toys were named after her. So, too, would be a gold mining company and a huge mill in Magnolia.

Five years after her return, on a writing assignment in the Midwest, Bly met millionaire Robert Seaman, a 72 year-old hardware manufacturer. They were married after a four-day courtship in April, 1895. He was old enough to be her grandfather.

According to *Brilliant Bylines, A Biographical Anthology of Notable Newspaperwomen in America,* Bly was considered a "golddigger" who simply married Seaman for his money. Little did her critics know that she and her husband would actually begin a search for gold of their own.

Seaman had many investments. At the time of his marriage with Bly, one of his most recent was the Keystone mill site at Magnolia, a few miles south of Boulder Canyon. A few weeks after their wedding, Robert Seaman and Elizabeth Cochrane Seaman (Nellie Bly) incorporated the Nellie Bly Gold Mining and Reduction Company with four other directors. Capital stock of one million dollars was divided into one hundred thousand shares of stock worth ten dollars per share. The stated purpose was to mine and mill gold ore.

The company then built the elaborate and expensive Nellie Bly Mill. It was at the height of its operation in 1898 and processed gold ore from the Keystone and nearby Kekionga mines. The Seamans' permanent home at the time was New York City. It's not known whether Nellie Bly ever visited her namesake, but given her interest in travel and taste for adventure, it's likely that she did.

Robert Seaman died in 1904, and Bly took over his various businesses. Eventually she invested her savings in Austria, only to lose them during the World War. Bly died of pneumonia in 1922. All that's left today as a reminder of this noted journalist are some stock prospectuses and the mill's ruins, hidden from view on private property.

In 1903, mining was renewed in the Magnolia area. The Great Western Mining, Milling and Sampling Company opened the Anna Clara and adjoining claims. A year later a reporter stated, "We feel that we can recommend it as a good prospective property, one in which it would be safe for one to invest his money with a view to receiving returns in the future, and from the present appearances it will not be long although the company is making no glittering promises of the get-rich-quick class."

UPPER BOULDER CANYON

Boulder Canyon competed for its share of the tourist trade. In 1920, Secretary of the Boulder Commercial Association (later the Boulder Chamber of Commerce) Frank Eckel built a lodge in Boulder Canyon at Rogers Park.

"Perhaps the most interesting thing about Eckel's," stated the hotel's literature, "is the old Black Hawk Indian Trail, which, long before white men came in, served as the communicating link between the great plains and the hunting grounds of Middle Park, beyond the Continental Divide. This Trail leads directly past the hotel door, crosses Middle Boulder Creek at Eckel's Ford, skirts the old Indian camp ground, and then abruptly ascends the thousand-foot slope to the south, and loses itself in the maze of ridges and canons on the way to Middle Park. The Trail is clearly marked, deeply worn into the rocky soil by the feet of the numberless Indians and ponies who threaded it in by-gone days."

The brochure boasted of "good food and good beds," but also provided its guests with "electric lights, hot and cold baths, and all of the conveniences that money can buy." There were sixteen guest rooms, and the dining room held fifty people. The hotel also claimed to have "bright and sparkling days, nights always cool enough to demand blankets," and "air filled with the scent of pine and balsam and the perfume of a thousand mountain wild flowers."

A 1920 *Daily Camera* article was entitled, "Frank Eckel and Wife Ready With Chicken Dinners." The entree was said to have been so good it would melt in your mouth. Room and board cost three dollars and up per day.

Just up the road was the "Perfect Tree," so named because

the spruce tapered symmetrically from base to tip. From even before the turn of the twentieth century, it became a destination for hikers and picnickers. In the 1930s, a concrete picnic table was placed as close as possible for passing motorists. The table is still there, but the tree, estimated to have reached approximately four hundred years, finally fell over and died.

The Perfect Tree ca. 1900. Author's collection.

WARD WAKES UP

"Ward is no longer a sleepy, rotting, dead town," wrote an optimistic newspaper reporter when the first train chugged into the struggling mining camp. The residents cheered, mine foremen and millmen blew their whistles, and miners scattered in all directions setting off blasts of dynamite which echoed off the mountainsides.

The reporter continued, "[Ward] feels the stimulus of the greedy hunt for gold and is roused into activity by the locomotive whistle. It has good hotels, a schoolhouse, two churches, fine buildings and stores, and is putting on metropolitan airs with modern improvements."

Much of western Boulder County was founded on mining, and Ward was no exception. Like all the mining towns, it had its ups and downs, but it came of age with the railroad.

Ward's initial gold discoveries predated the silver strike in Caribou. Then, in 1872, gold combined with tellurium was found in Gold Hill. This started the "telluride boom" that extended from Jamestown to Magnolia and included Sunshine, Salina, Wallstreet, and other gold mining camps. The mining industry was important enough to demand a railroad. Beginning in 1883, the Greeley, Salt Lake & Pacific ran its narrow gauge trains up and down Four Mile Canyon.

In 1898, under the ownership of the Colorado &

Northwestern, the railroad was extended from Sunset to Ward. The train ride from Boulder covered twenty-six and one-half miles. Passengers climbed four thousand feet in elevation to 9,450 feet above sea level. The special opening day round-trip fare was one dollar and thirty cents. Over three hundred and fifty people, including dignitaries, arrived on three special trains. From a speakers' rostrum, decked with spruce boughs, Colorado Governor Alva Adams spoke of the importance of gold and silver mining and of transportation being the measure of the wealth of the mines.

The year the railroad reached Ward was also the year that the Chautauqua Association was founded in Boulder. The cultural and educational summer "camp" was patronized mostly by Texans who longed for the beauty and climate of Colorado. Railroad excursions to Ward were one of their most popular activities.

Some of the tourists got off between Sunset and Gold Hill station to spend the day at Mont Alto. At this railroad-owned picnic pavilion, later moved to Glacier Lake, ladies in long dresses and big hats joined men in three-piece suits as they hiked, played baseball, drank beer, and enjoyed the beauty of the mountains.

Others continued on the train in order to spend two hours in Ward. During their brief, but intense, visit, the excursionists swarmed the hillsides, picked flowers, packed the restaurants, and took underground mine tours.

As usual, there were hotels for those who wished to stay overnight. One was the Albany, run by Uriah McClancy. Others included the Utica Hotel, Sulphide Inn, Sargent's Boarding House, and the Cottage House.

The Hotel McClancy was in Ward's business district and was the origin of the town's biggest fire. Carnegie Branch Library for Local History, Boulder Historical Society collection.

The Albany Hotel had been renamed the Hotel McClancy as early as 1892. Two rooms were set aside for travelers, but the rest were rented by miners who slept in three shifts of eight hours each. By the end of the nineteenth century, the McClancy was the largest and most popular hotel in Ward.

On January 24, 1900, the McClancy Hotel achieved additional notoriety as the origin of Ward's biggest fire. About one o'clock in the morning Mrs. M. J. McClancy discovered a fire in an ashcan next to the building.

"Had she a bucket of water handy," wrote a reporter, "it could have been easily extinguished, but before she could hunt up a bucket and pump it full of water, the flames had gained such headway that her bucket was useless. The wind was blowing a gale, and the flames soon swept across the street and the city was doomed. With neither water works nor a fire company, the people became desperate. Nothing could be done but try to save the furniture and goods."

Fifty-two mine whistles sounded the alarm. Women and children huddled on the hillsides as the fire burned unchecked for six hours. It was unseasonably warm, as a Chinook wind of hurricane force pushed down from the Continental Divide. Attempts to extinguish the fire were futile until a rare shift in the wind came with the first light of dawn. For a few seconds, the flames shot straight up, then retreated over the area already burned.

Ward was a disaster. Few businesses had escaped destruction. Residents spent the night drenching the schoolhouse and the Congregational Church with buckets of water and wet blankets and quilts. These two landmarks were saved along with the residential sections behind them. Both are duly recorded on the National Register of Historic Places. Today the school building houses the town hall, library, and post office.

After the fire, much of Ward was rebuilt. Smoke stacks from the mines and the ribbons of steam from the hoists and compressors were visible reminders of the activities underground. Unlike the dismal situation in Eldora, mining in Ward really prospered after the arrival of the railroad. Finally the trains could easily transport the ore to mills and smelters while they hauled in coal to provide a cheap alternative to wood for the steam-powered equipment in the mines. Livery rigs met the incoming trains. Prominent mining engineers from all over the country came to visit the mines while Eastern capitalists were treated like royalty in hopes they would invest their fortunes. Mine owners, suppliers, and tourists also arrived and needed a place to stay.

With so much of the former business district still in ashes, the C & N and the Columbia Hotels were built to fill the demand. Old-timers recalled lots of piano and Victrola playing at both of these hotels, with people dancing and enjoying themselves in the evenings. Orchestras came up on the train from Boulder to add to the good times.

The C & N Hotel was built a few months after Ward's big fire. Carnegie Branch Library for Local History, Boulder Historical Society collection.

The C & N Hotel was built in May, 1900, just uphill from the Congregational Church. It was named in memory of five men who were killed in a snowslide while constructing the Colorado & Northwestern railroad. The hotel was first run by Mrs. M. F. Thompson who had previously operated a boarding house the railroad men had used as their headquarters.

The Hotel Columbia was named for the Columbia gold lode. Carnegie Branch Library for Local History, Boulder Historical Society collection.

In 1901, the Hotel Columbia was built below the church and closer to the business district. In 1916, Emma and Albert Fairhurst purchased the hotel which continued to be popular with tourists.

Emma Fairhurst in front of her fireplace. Carnegie Branch Library for Local History, Boulder Historical Society collection.

The lobby in the Hotel Columbia held a glass case of ore specimens from nearby mines. An oil painting hung on the wall along with photographs of Ward's mines and miners. The focus of the room, however, was the fireplace made of gold and silver ore. On the mantel was a gold pan with rocks containing gold.

Author Forest Crossen interviewed Emma Fairhurst in 1949. At the time of the interview, the hotel was still open for business. Mrs. Fairhurst explained that she first got the idea for the fireplace while her husband was still alive. She told him that she wished there was some convenient way for the excursionists to see specimens from surrounding mines. In her interview she added,

"After Mr. Fairhurst passed away, in 1920, I was lonely, so I decided to do what we'd talked about so much. Mining men here contributed the ore specimens and some are very high-grade. [One piece] came from the Graphic mine in Magnolia and took two International Fair prizes, one at Omaha and one at Paris. It has been gratifying through the years to see the way people enjoy this fireplace. I've had members of three generations of the same family here to see it."

By 1919, Ward's gold mining had become unprofitable. The mountain railroad lost money even before a flood washed out many of its bridges. Both the southern line to Eldora and the northern line to Ward were abandoned. The hotels directed their attention to tourists who came in automobiles instead.

Brochures in the 1920s called the C & N Hotel "The Old Reliable." By the 1930s, it advertised its wonderful views from its verandah as well as baths and electric lights. In the early 1960s, the two-story frame C & N Hotel was in such poor condition that it was condemned and torn down. During the process, a family member wrote nostalgically of stopping to read calling cards and old newspapers while prying loose the wall boards.

The Hotel Columbia advertised modern conveniences, special trout and chicken dinners, and guides furnished by request for glacier trips. In its own brochure, the traveler was told,

"Evenings pass quickly at the Columbia. You'll enjoy the flicker of the firelight and the crackle of the logs in the big fireplace. This too is unlike any you have ever seen, for it is made entirely of specimens of ore from mines in this district; some of the richest gold and silver mines in the world are represented. Your welcome at the Columbia Hotel will be a real Western one. We want you to make this your vacation home. Our rooms are spotless and airy, perfumed by the pines and balsams, and your sleep will be refreshing beyond belief. The meals are home-cooked and carefully served, just the kind you want and enjoy after a day in your motor, on horseback, or afoot."

Guests were directed to climb or horseback to Isabelle Glacier where one could "snow ball to your heart's content, and gather wild flowers for your table as you journey back to dinner of mountain trout fresh from the icy waters." Both hotels also offered furnished cottages. The Pines Cafe sold fresh bakery goods, lunches, and had a soda fountain.

Emma Fairhurst died in Ward in 1950. The hotel was inherited by her niece Hazel Schmoll. The building was used as a museum for a short time but never again as a hotel. In January, 1968, hundreds of antiques from the hotel burned in a nearby garage where they had been stored. Today the Columbia Hotel building stands vacant, and the balcony has been removed.

Stapp's Lake Lodge was one of the first resorts to open in the Ward area following the arrival of the railroad. Guests were welcome to hike and fish. Above, some of the cabins. Below, inside the lodge.
Courtesy *Daily Camera.*

After the arrival of the railroad, the area around Ward also drew tourists. Stapp's Lake Lodge, northwest of Ward, opened to the public in approximately 1903. Owner Isaac Stapp met his guests at the Ward depot and took them in his horse-drawn wagon to his three hundred-acre retreat. Later his sons John and Bill took over the business. The lodge was furnished with homemade rustic furniture and surrounded with fifteen two-unit cabins, each with its own woodstove.

If they wished, guests fished for trout in three of the five lakes stocked from the resort's private hatchery. At the end of the day, they turned in their catch and had their own fish for dinner in the dining room.

The Stapp's Lake resort operated as a dude ranch in the 1950s. Then, in the early 1960s, it was sold to G. B. Henderson who started the Alexander Dawson Foundation, owner of a private school north of Lafayette. The Stapp's Lakes property was used at the time as a children's summer camp.

In 1988 Stapp's Lake was sold again, this time to the monastic community named the Sacred Mountain Ashram, formerly located near Gold Hill. In a newspaper interview at the time of the sale, Swami Amar Jyoti said that the land offered relatively untouched peace for meditation and contemplation and communication with God and nature."

Another Ward area resort was Stony Point Lodge, now Tahosa Boy Scout Camp on Tumblesom Lake just off the Beaver Reservoir Road. Ogalalla Lodge was also nearby, on the road to Estes Park, now the Peak to Peak Highway. The Lodge of the Pines was on the old stage road between Ward and Jamestown. Farther to the north was Hazel Schmoll's Range View Ranch.

Immediately north of the Ward turn-off is the road to Brainard Lake, once the location for Camp Audubon. Opposite the Millsite Inn restaurant is the road to Gold Lake. This resort, currently open to the public, was once a girls' camp.

REBIRTH OF NEDERLAND

For years, prospectors in the Nederland area cursed "the damned black iron" that kept them from discovering new sources of silver and gold. The ore they found turned out to be rich in tungsten which eventually put Nederland in the national spotlight.

In 1904, William "Billy" Loach and A. G. McKenna formed the Wolf Tongue Mining Company, named for the elements wolfram and tungsten. The partners took over the old Caribou silver mill, in Nederland, and converted it to the milling of tungsten. Concentrates then were sent to the Firth Sterling Steel Company in McKeesport, Pennsylvania.

Tungsten mining brought Nederland a new lease on life. As the population rose, more and more people needed supplies. In August, 1905, Wallace L. Tanner moved to Nederland from Boulder. At first he tried his hand at mining, surveying, and even gambling in the local saloons. In a later interview he stated, "I'd never seen a roulette wheel before, but we got to playing it. We made wages, and I thought I had a way to make a living. But it didn't last."

Finally Tanner found his niche and opened a grocery store. He picked up his groceries, meats, and mining supplies at the closest railroad stop, in Cardinal, two miles west of Nederland.

Once a week he harnessed up his team and made deliveries from Caribou to Rollinsville. In later years, his Ford pick-up truck took him to the same communities. When his brothers, Ira and Silas, joined him, in 1913, the business became known as Tanner Brothers.

Several disastrous fires plagued Nederland around this time. A stove-pipe overheated in Bill Scott's General Store, on the southwest corner of Bridge and First Streets near today's visitor center. After the store burned down, flying embers jumped across the street igniting other commercial buildings. Accounts vary, but most agree that many of the men were in Boulder either doing their banking or attending a court case. Women and children formed bucket brigades, but there was little they could do to control the blaze. The few men who remained in town carried a piano down to the creek and covered it with wet quilts in their effort to save it.

Loach, who had led the town in the development of the tungsten industry, reflected many years later, "Much of it I wouldn't want to go through again, but there were some things that I wish we had more of today. Like the way people helped each other in those early days. If a man were injured or had sickness in the family, everybody helped. Then, too, people had more hopes for the future. I think they got more out of life."

Besides the growing tungsten industry, Nederland received an economic boost in 1909 and 1910 when the Colorado Power Company built Barker Dam and "Lake Nederland." In order to haul in heavy equipment, the Denver Boulder & Western railroad even built a spur line from Sulfide Flats, east of Eldora, to the main construction camp just below the dam site. A gravity line, over eleven miles long, transported the water from the lake into Kossler Reservoir, then dropped it through a penstock to the Boulder Hydroelectric Plant in Boulder Canyon.

A temporary spur line ran from Sulphide Flats to the construction site of Barker Dam. The two-story hotel in this stylized drawing of the proposed town east of Eldora was never completed, and the expected metropolis never materialized. Author's collection.

Shortly afterwards, the first "auto stage," a twelve-passenger Stanley Steamer, managed to complete the drive from Boulder to Nederland. The single-lane wagon road had remained essentially unimproved since it was quickly-constructed after the silver strike in Caribou. Then, in 1913, recently-elected Commissioner Jack Clark came up with the revolutionary idea of improving the road up Boulder Canyon by bringing in a crew of convicts from the state penitentiary.

After a summer of backbreaking labor, the road gang's

efforts were greatly appreciated. Editor L. C. Paddock of the Boulder *Daily Camera* raved about the road and wrote, "Have you been through Boulder Canon [original spelling] this year? It is one of the safest mountain auto trips if your driver will only toot his horn and exercise common sense precautions. While it affords gorgeous views of the snowcapped range, with mine and mills in operation, it presents the handsomest of all lakes east of the Great range, water a mile and a quarter in length and of half that width, with glorious pine groves, and a variety not afforded by any other canon in Colorado that can be reached in a day's ride from any center of population. It's worth telling the world about."

The crew of convicts was welcome, but transients in Nederland were not tolerated. In May, 1915, the *Boulder County Miner* newspaper noted, "On Friday of last week a band of about thirty gypsies with six wagons came to town and camped by the creek back of Crawford's house. Mayor Lawrence told them to leave within an hour or he would lock them, kids, wagons, and all, in our two by four jail. They left. The day was damp and chilly. Slim Caywood, Bill Nolan, Bill Harris, Dr. Frontz, and Silas Tanner caught bad colds watching the performance."

Next came the "usual number of sharps and vagabonds who prey on new mining camps." The Nederland town Marshal put a group of them to work improving the city streets. A newspaper report stated, "Nederland has no intention to be known as a wild and woolly western mining camp. People are progressive and welcome the good miners and clean investors who are coming to join them. After the street work is completed, however, the toughs and bums will not find the Marshal waiting at the city limits to welcome them with a pick and shovel. He will then have a club stuffed with tungsten and give it weight and authority."

Nederland did want the tourists. Travelers had "discovered" the town during nearby Eldora's period of mining activity. As Nederland began to grow again, it made a new effort at self-promotion by calling itself a town of "snowy mountains, pine-clad hills and gulches, clear creeks and boulders, fish, elk, baseball games, movies, and dances."

A group of local businessmen formed the Nederland Fish and Game Club in 1913. They bought fifty thousand fish to stock Barker Reservoir, then called Lake Nederland. An editor wrote, "It is a well-known fact that tourists will overcome almost any inconvenience of travel or surroundings to get to a place where fish can be caught in abundance. Nederland has the fish, it has splendid scenery and climate, plenty of amusements, interest as the center of the tungsten mining industry, most of the modern conveniences, and again, let us say, lots of trout. Let these things be known and we will have tourists."

According to a January 25, 1915, article in the *Boulder County Miner*, the Fish and Game Club sent personal invitations to over one thousand people asking them to purchase panoramic photographs of the lake and of Nederland. The plan was to distribute ten thousand advertising photographs to the Denver hotels and railroad depots. Whether or not this was done is unknown, as none of the photos have shown up in the usual research facilities.

Actively promoting the club was its secretary, "Fatty" Mills, who had moved to Nederland from Eldora. Author Geneva Meyring described him as a "gruff, lovable man." John

Valentine, who delivered hardware and mining supplies from Valentine's Hardware in Boulder said he was "as wide as he was tall." Under the direction of "the big chief," as Mills was called in the newspapers, workers cleared the upper end of the lake of brush in order to prevent their fish hooks from getting snagged. Then trails were built around the south shore.

To add wildlife to the area, thirteen elk were transported by train from Jackson Hole, Wyoming, to Nederland. Three died on the way. According to the newspaper, the rest sunned themselves on the south slope of the ridge west of the Wolf Tongue Mill. All the dogs in town were locked up for a period of ten days to prevent them from "worrying" the elk. The Fish and Game Club asked that residents also keep away from the elk until they got rested and used to their new home.

Whether Nederland's tourists came for fish and elk or for the scenery, they needed a place to stay, and the Antlers Hotel was open to accommodate them. The *Colorado Business Directory* advertised the hotel's location on the edge of the Lake Nederland. Hotel representatives met incoming trains at Cardinal while two daily automobile lines ferried people up the improved Boulder Canyon road in two Stanley Steamers and one gasoline-powered automobile.

Just when the town was encouraging tourism, it was on the verge of its biggest-ever mining boom. The War in Europe had greatly increased the demand for tungsten. By September, 1915, the *Boulder County Miner* announced, "Travel is unprecedented because of the boom in the tungsten camp, and the [stage] lines are doing a better business than in the very best of the tourist season. Nederland doubled in the last six months. There is not a vacant house in the town nor a vacant cabin in the district. It is difficult to find a room which can be rented. In every gulch and valley there are groups of tents and half the faces one sees are unfamiliar."

Miners, rudely awakened to make room for each other, lived in rooming houses which rented beds in eight-hour shifts. Twenty minutes were considered sufficient to eat a meal. According to one reporter, the only place to sleep was on the hillside "with the sky above you for a blanket."

As the winter approached, Reverend Currens, an enterprising minister, found a way to alleviate the housing problem and establish the Nederland Community Church at the same time. After the roof was on his new church building, the Reverend rented out spaces on the benches and the floor to miners with no other place to sleep.

During the tungsten boom, miners paid to sleep in this church, now called the Community Presbyterian Church. Photo by author, 1998.

McKenzie's Store (originally built by John Pickle as a Hardware Store), on the left, and Hetzer's Saloon, on the right, occupied the northwest corner of First and Bridge Streets when this photo was taken in 1897. Colin McKenzie is on the left with his two sons. The buildings burned down in one of the town's fires shortly after the turn of the twentieth century. Carnegie Branch Library for Local History, Boulder Historical Society collection.

NEDERLAND'S TUNGSTEN BOOM

Tungsten mining and activity in Nederland reached its peak from late 1915 through 1916. Author Forest Crossen vividly described the situation which created this demand,

"In far-off Europe, the armies of Germany and Austria-Hungary were locked in terrible combat with the Allies. The fields of France and Russia were blasted and blood-soaked. An ocean of supplies of all kinds was needed to keep these men killing each other. Munitions and arms they had to have, and for this manufacturing of high-speed tool steel was a must. Tungsten alloyed with steel produced a tool that would cut and continue to cut when hot."

The newspapers were full of developments on the War. "How the War Started" was succinctly explained in as follows:

"Austria got Hungary.
Turkey said they'd Servia.
Servia slipped on Greece
and broke up China."

Every mine, and nearly every prospect in the district, was said to be making money. Twenty-two mills processed the area's tungsten ores. The Wolf Tongue operated twenty-four hours per day, seven days per week, except for the Fourth of July, Thanksgiving, and Christmas. The Primos Mining & Milling Company, a few miles north of Nederland, at the town of Lakewood, was the largest tungsten mill in the world.

As the price of tungsten rose dramatically, new buildings in Nederland's commercial district went up almost overnight. Others changed hands and were wired for electricity. In one year, the population was said to have jumped from a few hundred to over three thousand. Automobiles clogged Boulder Canyon in the daytime while trucks hauled mining supplies at night.

In 1915, C. W. Blake bought a building on West First Street which became known as "Blake's Hall." "A peppery bunch of fiddlers" were brought in for dances and rickety folding chairs were set up for movies. Films at the time were short, fuzzy, and silent. They were projected onto a white sheet at the end of the room every Saturday night and often another night during the week. Some of the early titles included "Who Seeks Revenge" and "Bronco Billy and the Gambler." Another was called "Love, Loot, and Liquor."

The hall was also used by the "Sunshine Club," probably the same as the "Sunshine Society" of Eldora. The club's purpose was "to bring good cheer and material assistance to the destitute." Members of the service organization met in the hall to dance and play cards. Meetings were also held to form the Nederland Redman Band and to organize the town's baseball team. When the team lost one of its first games to the town of Superior, a less-than-sympathetic reporter called them "butterfingers and boneheads."

In 1916, Blake either sold or rented the building to "Shorty" Long who continued to show moving pictures. A sign out in front simply read "Theatre." Today the building is Nederland's Town Hall.

The Town Hall, on the right, was a movie theater and dance hall during the days of the tungsten boom. Photo by author, 1998.

At the time, Nederland's "City Hall" was located in a remodeled stable on the northwest corner of Bridge and 2nd Streets. Besides city business, it also hosted sermons including one by a missionary to Siam. An Easter cantata of forty singers performed "The Resurrection and the Life" which was attended by two hundred fifty people. In 1937, the City Hall building was replaced with Boulder County's stone maintenance garage.

Besides the Antlers, hotels in the boom days included the Hetzer, McRae, Lacer, and the Western Hotel run by "Cap" George Trollope and his wife. The Western was located on the northeast corner of Second and Johnson Streets. Boulder hardware merchant J. W. Valentine often stayed there on his visits to Nederland. He endured "Cap's" non-stop talking and relished

Mrs. Trollop's home-cooked meals.

As the price of tungsten rose in late 1915, Nederland filled with miners and investors. The men gathered, as they had always done, in saloons. Then, on January 1, 1916, Colorado Prohibition went into effect, four years before the whole country. Saloons became pool halls and advertised "soft drinks, cigars, confectionery, and pastime." Those who had to have their liquor sought out the illegal bootleggers.

Soft drinks and one theater weren't enough to entertain Nederland's increasing population, so, in the winter of 1915-1916, Blake and "Fatty" Mills built a new movie theater just east of the building now occupied by the Mountain People's Coop. Unlike "Shorty" Long's Theatre, the new one had comfortable seats and a sloping floor. Electric footlights shone on a handsomely-painted curtain which was lowered over the screen at the end of each performance. Brightly-painted mountain scenes decorated the side walls. Residents called the building "a credit to the town" and were saddened when it burned in the 1920s.

Because of a series of devastating fires, little remains of Nederland's early commercial buildings. Most were built during a burst in the economy which accompanied the tungsten boom.

A large two-story false-fronted building was erected in the winter of 1915-1916 on the site of the Pickel/McKenzie store and the small building next door. An upstairs rooming house was called the McRae Hotel. (With its three upstairs windows, the McRae is similar to, but not the same as the old Hetzer Saloon.) Downstairs were storage rooms for the Hub and other stores.

This photo was taken by Donald Kemp in April, 1916, and is well-captioned in his book, "Silver, Gold and Black Iron," published in 1960. Kemp stated, "Among the many hotels were the McRae, the two-story false front building at upper right; and the famed Hetzer House, dating back to the '70s, three doors beyond. Sandwiched between were 'Shorty' Long's elaborately-faced movie theatre (doing duty today as the Nederland Town Hall) and Tanner Brothers' grocery store. The McRae building survives and for many years was the Silver Dollar Tavern owned by R. C. (Dick) Murdock." (Don't confuse the McRae Hotel with Hetzer's Saloon on page 88.)
Carnegie Branch Library for Local History,
Boulder Historical Society collection.

Kemp failed to note the other buildings between the theatre and the Hetzer House. One is a hotel called the Lacer House, and the other may be the building now occupied by the Town Marshal. The Hetzer House was purchased in 1917 by John and Molly MacKenzie (note different spelling from the Colin McKenzie family) who renamed it and added a large addition. Molly was the daughter of Louise Jamieson, previous Hetzer House manager who also briefly managed the Gold Miner Hotel in Eldora.

The Mint Pool Hall replaced the building on the corner in Kemp's 1916 photo. The two-story building to the left (west) was the McRae Hotel. Another two-story building, which also fronted on Bridge Street, was built behind the pool hall. This large building contained storage rooms for Maupins Furniture store. Photo ca. 1919. Author's collection.

In 1934, after Prohibition was over, the Silver Dollar Tavern opened in the McRae Hotel building. This photograph was taken in the 1940s after the false-front had been removed. Carnegie Library for Local History, Boulder.

Above, the "Mint" was demolished and the two-story building behind it became Dick's Corner Service Station. The two front windows were added. Carnegie Branch Library for Local History, Boulder. *Below, these girls rode their burro downtown in the 1940s.* Photo courtesy Roberta Childers.

In 1998, the remodeled Silver Dollar Tavern is the home of One World Cafe. The theatre (Town Hall), next door was moved back from the street. The tavern building and the remodeled service station have become Wolf Tongue Square. Note the same two windows. Both photos by author, 1998.

In this 1909 photograph of East First Street, looking east, the Beach Block is the two-story building on the south (right) side of the street in the background. The building is no longer standing. The Pioneer Saloon building (not to be confused with today's Pioneer Inn) may be the same one occupied today by Off Her Rocker Antiques. The Nederland Mercantile was on the site of Scott's General Store. Both burned in early fires. Bridge Street ran between the Pioneer Saloon and the Nederland Mercantile. Widened route 119 covers this location today. Carnegie Branch Library for Local History, Boulder Historical Society collection.

After the turn of the twentieth century, commercial buildings also occupied both sides of East First Street, east of Bridge Street. One was the Beach "Block," meaning it had two or more storefronts. The main part of the building, which burned by 1915, was two-story and contained Fish and Game Club President W. E. Binder's confectionery and stationery store.

In this 1911 photo, the two-story Beach Block is to the west (right) of Nederland's post office. Bucking Brown Trout Company, at 26 East First Street, either is the old post office building or is on the site of the old post office. Carnegie Branch Library for Local History, Boulder Historical Society collection.

Stage coach driver William DeVoss hauled the mail from the Cardinal railroad station during the height of the mining activity in 1915 and 1916. He carried forty-five to fifty sacks, plus packages, per day. When he pulled into Nederland there was always a crowd lined up a block long waiting for their mail.

After the Beach Block was destroyed by fire, "Fatty" Mills built the one-story Hub Store in half of the remaining space. The store sold boys' and men's clothing. The building remained at least through the 1940s, but is no longer standing. It was located immediately west of today's Bucking Brown Trout Company. The Hub Store may also have been the location of Mills & Mills, a store later owned by "Fatty" Mills's son and daughter.

The buildings on the north (left) side of East First Street, in the 1909 photograph, have both been replaced. During 1916, Tanner Brothers Grocery moved a frame saloon (probably the one on the northwest corner of Bridge and First Streets in the photograph on page 93) across the street to the northeast corner and used the building for the final location of Tanner Brothers Groceries. The store burned ca. 1947. Robert Childers opened a supermarket in a new building on the same site.

Little is known of the remaining north side of East First Street except that the oldest buildings date from the tungsten boom. They probably are among the ten to twelve new buildings erected in the winter of 1915 - 1916. The *Boulder County Miner* stated, at the time, "The town council is taking a very wise and progressive policy in directing the character of building and preventing the defacement of the pretty place by rude shacks and inferior structures. The buildings are all good."

Above, East First Street, looking east, is quite different today. Mountain Peoples' Coop is on the right, where Hodgson Transfer used to be.

Below, Nature's Own, at 5 East First Street, is on the last site of Tanner Brothers Groceries which was replaced with a new supermarket built by Robert Childers in the late 1940s. Both photos by author, 1998.

Residences had been built on the original town lots platted in 1877 and in Beach's Addition laid out in 1908. Suddenly, in 1916, new subdivisions enlarged the town. Houses popped up like mushrooms.

Then, much faster than it started, the tungsten boom was over. The first indication of hard times to come was the flu epidemic in the fall of 1918. The assistant manager of the Primos mill wrote to his manager, "The influenza first appeared in Nederland about October 1st. Its spread was so rapid [that] by October 18th the entire district was demoralized. On the 16th and 17th our mill crew was down to one shift, and on the 18th we shut down the mill and all mines except the Quaker, as we could not get men enough for even one shift. All other mines in the district were shut down. Out of our mine crew of seventy-five men, fifteen men have died. There were, however, no deaths among our mill crew although practically every man contracted the disease."

The Antlers Hotel was converted into a temporary hospital. Nurses lined the large porch with cots. As the sick slowly recovered, they learned of the Armistice signed on November 11, 1918. The boom had collapsed as the wartime demand for tungsten was over.

Nederland looked to what it had done before and promoted tourism. The Nederland Commercial Association again pushed its fishing. The group wrote in their travel brochures, "The lakes are heavily stocked with many varieties of trout and offer unequaled sport. Other lakes, scattered over the wild and broken country clear to the Divide, offer added inducements to the seeker for good angling. Even if you don't fish it's great to spend the summer where the fishing is good."

Some tourists slept under the pines with conveniences unknown to the prospectors of the boom days. A free campground, called an auto park, was set up to accommodate over a hundred cars, complete with city water, comfort stations, a dance hall, and massive stone fireplaces equipped with grates for cooking.

In 1920, James A. Lang bought the Antlers Hotel and renamed it Langcrest. It was advertised it as "A newly-refurnished family hotel on the crest of a hill overlooking Nederland Lake and within sight of miles of the Snowy Range." At least one guest came from as far away as Florence, Italy. A few others were from New York, Houston, and Chicago, but there also were many from Boulder.

In the mid-1930s, even Denver's *Rocky Mountain News* encouraged tourism in the Nederland area. An article boasted that its "mountains are highest, canons deepest, and glaciers largest." At the turn in the road at Barker Dam, the writer spoke of viewing "one of the most magnificent panoramas of the western mountain country."

The MacKenzie House (formerly Hetzer Hotel) was the last of Nederland's historic hotels to stay open. It was said to have been "much patronized by traveling men, autoists, and fishermen." It burned in yet another fire on December 4, 1939.

In 1932, the Antlers/Langcrest Hotel was purchased by the Catholic Daughters of America and converted into a summer camp for girls. In 1935, the Chapel of St. Rita was built next door for the campers. By 1961, the old hotel building had deteriorated and was torn down to make room for parking. The chapel, above, was enlarged and has become today's St. Rita's Catholic Church. Photo by author, 1998.

This view of Nederland was taken after the stone maintenance garage was built in 1937 and before the MacKenzie Hotel, on the left, burned in 1939. The Silver Dollar Tavern still has its false-front. The town hall building has been moved to its recessed location. Bridge Street no longer crosses the creek in its original north-south direction, but has been rerouted slightly to the west. (Compare to the photograph on page 14.)
Carnegie Branch Library for Local History,
Boulder Historical Society collection.

Mrs. Martin, longtime proprietress of the Gold Miner Hotel, also ran Mrs. Martin's Restaurant on the south (right) side of Eldorado Avenue. On the north side of the street is the Eldora Hotel. This view in early-day Eldora is looking east. (Compare to photograph on page 28.) Courtesy Earl and Barbara Bolton.

ELDORA THROUGH THE YEARS

The end of the railroad didn't stop tourists from going to Eldora. They came in automobiles instead.

Sarah Martin stayed on at the Gold Miner Hotel into the early 1920s. She also ran "Mrs. Martin's Restaurant" whose pancakes were described by at least one customer as "a little hard, the milk thin, and the butter thinner."

In 1924, Elizabeth Rearick and Elizabeth Penrose rented the Eldora cabins formerly called Woodland Park Lodge. They decided to open a "vacation camp" with sleeping quarters, home-cooked meals, and guide service for day hikes. Elizabeth Rearick eventually pursued other projects, but Elizabeth Penrose built additional cabins and changed the name to Penrose Lodge.

By this time, Arapaho Glacier was receiving national publicity. There was no easy way to reach the glacier, but there were two routes which got tourists close enough to hike or ride a pack animal the rest of the way. One was the road to Rainbow Lakes and the other was the road through Eldora. Drivers of the "Glacier Route Automobiles" met the electrically-powered interurban and other incoming trains in Boulder, then drove tourists to one of these starting points.

In 1925, Eldora's winter population was seventeen while its summer population was three thousand five hundred.

This 1925 view of Eldora, above, is dominated by the two-story schoolhouse to the right of center. The Gold Miner Hotel, also two-story, but much smaller, is to the left of center. Below, a group of travelers posed in front of one of Eldora's stores. Both photos courtesy Earl and Barbara Bolton.

The Glacier Route company advertised prompt service, courteous and careful drivers, and large, roomy cars. Fare from Boulder to Eldora was two dollars.

Once the tourists reached Eldora, the late Jim Sewell led pack trips up the road to the Fourth of July shafthouse, then on to the top of "Arapaho Saddle." From there they could climb South Arapaho Peak or descend onto the glacier itself. "People who'd never been on a horse or a burro used to go," he recalled in a later interview. "People who'd never been on a jackass in their lives wouldn't get on a horse. They had to ride a burro. High-toned people. Lots o'times people from the East would get up on Arapaho Peak and get sick. Those with heart trouble weren't supposed to go up there, but they would. When they'd get sick on me way up there I'd have a time. They'd be so limber they couldn't sit on a burro or horse, so I'd rig up a litter I carried. It was just a canvas stretcher between two long poles. I'd put two burros, one ahead of the other and stick the poles through the saddle stirrups. The people could ride along right between 'em. I had whiskey, but some of 'em wouldn't take as much as a spoonful. If they'd taken it, they would have snapped out of it. I had other stuff along too — medicine, but whiskey always seemed to do the most good."

Soon more and more travelers came to Eldora in their own cars. They stayed at the Gold Miner Hotel, the Penrose Lodge, rented housekeeping cabins, or built seasonal cabins of their own.

Then the Great Depression brought the growth of the tourist industry to a halt, not just in Eldora, but all over the state and the nation. Yet the *Eldora Echo,* published in 1934 and 1935, mentions the still-open Gold Miner Hotel.

Frank J. Anderson was the owner at the time and rented out a few rooms in the summertime. In 1934, with the help of the community, he built a "club room" onto the northeast side of the building. Unlike the rest of the hotel, the logs are milled on the top, bottom, and interior, but left rounded on the exterior.

The club room was the largest room in town. Anderson added a piano and made the room available for community gatherings and events including —

Weekly meetings of the Eldora Social and Civic Club.
Ladies Day luncheons where "the afternoon was spent in playing cards, chatting, and sewing."
Evening "gatherings" and family parties.
Dances and weddings.
A talk on Africa and South America by Dr. Hilda Heller.
"Needed medical services" offered by Dr. Carrie Anderson from Nederland.
Christmas parties with Frank Anderson as Santa Claus.

In 1935, Helena Nelson managed the Gold Miner Hotel. Nelson advertised "moderate and reasonable prices" for "clean and sanitary sleeping rooms, home-cooked food, and continuous service." She also specialized in private parties, including luncheons, teas, and dinners with home-baked pastries, cookies, doughnuts, and cakes. Lunches were put up at the Gold Miner for "outgoing parties" who looked through the classified ads for "tramping shoes."

In 1935, Eldora consisted of two hundred cabins, many available to rent. Besides the Gold Miner Hotel and the Penrose Lodge, the town's business section consisted of four grocery stores, two wood and coal dealers, a cafe, a garage, and an ice dealer. Al's Place advertised dry goods, hardware, and Gates tires. Olsen's had milk for nine cents and dinners for fifty cents. "Nice and clean" cabins were available up the road in Hessie for those who wanted to fish and go horseback riding. The Lilly Stables offered saddle and pack horses, wood, ice, and cabins.

Twice a week the McNeil Haney vegetable wagon made its rounds. Another supplier, M. Forte, delivered vegetables grown in Nederland. Model Laundry from Boulder would pick up and deliver clothes on Tuesdays and Fridays. A "licensed driver" was even available for private scenic tours.

The C-BAR-E stables in Nederland replaced old-timer Jim Sewell and charged fifty cents per hour, or three dollars and fifty cents per day, for pack to trips to Arapaho Glacier, Woodland Lake, James Peak, Lost Lake, or Corona. The stables also managed the annual Nederland Rodeo which featured steer riding, bulldogging, wild cow milking, and bronco busting, as well as a free-for-all race, roping-horse race, trick roping, calf roping, and cow-horse relays.

Forest rangers supervised boys in building trails out of old wagon roads. In 1935 the crews worked in the vicinity of Corona, Woodland Flat, and on the way to the Fourth of July shafthouse. The same year the federal government raised the price of gold from just over twenty dollars to thirty-five dollars. Mayor William Harpel reopened his Enterprise mine on Spencer Mountain.

By then, only a handful of people lived in Eldora year around. Two of them were teenagers Philip Rouse and William Gross who published the *Eldora Echo* during the summers of 1934 and 1935. Their definition of a resort was "a place where natives charge summer visitors enough in three months to live happily the other nine," yet single copies of "the coolest newspaper in the Rocky Mountain Region" were only three cents, while a summer subscription cost only twenty-five cents.

The *Eldora Echo* listed everyone's arrival in town. The Harry Cox family owned the "Wolverine," while the J. Paul Leonards stayed in "Rest-a-While." Others reopened cabins including "Glen Echo", "Wee Hoose," "Emporia", "Retreat", "Rocky Ledge", "Pinehurst", "Junior", "Sunnyside", "Call O' The Wild", "Canon View", "Sunkist", "Happy Valley Lodge", "Pooh's Corner", "Cloudland", "Nebraska", and "Wild Wood."

The teenagers' newspaper reported that the "old Durand Store," called an "eyesore," was torn down in 1935. Furnishings were sold at "unheard of prices." In the days before people even thought about historic preservation, the store's disappearance was referred to as "the town improvement."

Short editorials lashed out against the dump, called "a disgrace to the town." Others commented on the poor condition of the roads. One visitor left his mark with the following sentiments —

"There are roads that make you happy,
And roads that make you sad,
There are roads that make you loving,
And roads that make you mad.
Of all the endless journeys to tour America first,
There's one that leads to Eldora, which, like Hell,
could not be worse!"

Eldora's residents had not been invaded by large groups of people since the excursionists came on the railroad. Then, in 1939, two hundred people in automobiles passed through town in a caravan. That was the year the Boulder Chamber of Commerce held its first annual hike to the overlook site above Arapaho Glacier.

Along with Boulder's mayor was the city manager, the superintendent of schools, the president and secretary of the Chamber of Commerce, several members of the University faculty, the Boulder County Commissioners, a state senator, newspaper reporters, and many prominent business and professional men and women. After they carpooled up Boulder Canyon, they continued on through Eldora to a base camp at the Fourth of July campground. Breakfast was served before the hike began.

Upon reaching the overlook, the Rocky Mountain Rescue Group presented a rock climbing exhibition on the final leg of the climb up South Arapaho Peak. Some of the hikers descended onto the glacier to slide and throw snowballs. After they returned, the group headed back to base camp for a hot dinner, then drove through Eldora on their way home.

Organized hikes continued through 1976 and included over fourteen thousand people. Some stopped at Eldora's Fountain Restaurant, run by Robert Childers who also owned a grocery store in Nederland.

By the time Helen "D." and Francis Dunnagan bought the Gold Miner Hotel, in 1956, the town had a small grocery store, a motel, post office, yarn shop, and a few rental cabins. The few residents went to Nederland or Boulder for most of their groceries.

Above, the Fountain Restaurant was run by Nederland grocer Robert Childers in the 1940s. Below, wild flowers decorated each table in the family-run restaurant. Both photos courtesy Roberta Childers.

For the next ten years, the Dunnagans used the hotel building as a summer home for family and friends. However, they made the club room available for town meetings. In 1967, the family sold the building to Harold and Dottie Martin who also used it as a private residence. The Martins remodeled the small guest rooms to five larger ones. Floor patterns on the second floor reveal the locations of original wall partitions. In 1979, Dwight Souter and Jean Bell reopened the Gold Miner as a Bed and Breakfast. It has remained a Bed and Breakfast ever since.

From the front and west side, the Gold Miner Hotel looks the same as it did when it was built in the winter of 1897-1898. Photo by author, 1996.

The clapboard front and the gingerbread trim on the porch have withstood a century of time. The building is still in use and, except for the club-room addition, still looks the same. A one-story porch with four turned posts and two more against the wall extends across the front, just as it did on the day it was built. In 1997 the Boulder County Commissioners approved the Gold Miner Hotel as a Boulder County Landmark. Much of the town is designated a national historic district, but the hotel also claims individual recognition on the National Register of Historic Places.

IN CONCLUSION

Today's travelers still visit the Nederland area to hike, fish, and enjoy the mountain scenery. In fact, by 1978, so many visitors had come to the mountains west of Eldora and Ward that 73,391 acres of land in Boulder and Grand Counties — part of the Roosevelt National Forest, Arapaho National Forest, and 500 acres of Rocky Mountain National Park — were set aside as the Indian Peaks Wilderness.

Named for the Arapaho, Arikaree, Navajo, Apache, Shoshoni, Kiowa, and Pawnee Peaks within its boundaries, this undeveloped area spans the Continental Divide and extends from Rocky Mountain National Park, to the north, to Rollins Pass, to the south.

The wilderness is managed by the United States Forest Service which provides permits for camping and group use, places limitations on fires and livestock, requires leash control of dogs, and prohibits bicycles, vehicles, and all motorized equipment. Unlike the early excursionists who rode the narrow gauge railroad and gathered huge bouquets, today's tourists are not allowed to pick the masses of colorful wild flowers.

Besides the Indian Peaks area, locals and tourists alike have spread out all over western Boulder County. Horseback riding and pack trips are still in demand. An increasing number of visitors have taken up mountain biking, while others still enjoy an afternoon drive.

Not all visitors come in the summer. Today's tourists have added downhill and cross-country skiing to their list of outdoor activities. Particularly popular are the trails in the vicinity of Lake Eldora and Brainard Lake and those of Eldora Mountain Resort outside Nederland.

While the mountains are enjoyed more than ever, only a few old-timers can recall the days of the railroad. The narrow gauge Denver, Boulder & Western to Ward and Eldora was abandoned in 1919. Tracks were pulled up, and, over time, the rights of way were used for new homes. When the Moffat Tunnel opened in 1928, travelers were rushed through the Continental Divide instead of viewing the spectacular scenery from the "top of the world." A few Colorado communities, such as Silverton and Leadville, have reconstructed their railroads. Perhaps one day the sound of a train whistle will again echo through Boulder County's mountain canyons.

Mining, like railroading, may also be part of our past. After Nederland's tungsten boom was over, China captured most of the world market. Gold mining all but disappeared in the 1920s, but was revitalized in the 1930s when the price of gold was raised from twenty-seven dollars and sixty cents to thirty-five dollars per ounce. World War II put an end to most of Boulder County's gold output, but the Korean War created a new demand for tungsten.

Although a few gold mines are still open on an occasional basis, environmental restrictions and a lack of operating capital plague the local mining industry. The future is unknown while history often repeats itself. Mining booms and busts have been as unpredictable as the fires which once swept through the mining towns.

Fire danger is less in mountain towns today due to organized fire protection districts and fire codes. While the incidence of structure fires has gone down, the number of forest fires has gone up. As more homes are built in forested areas and the backcountry receives more extensive use, the threat of fire increases for the next century.

Most of the historic accommodations *Inn and Around Nederland* are in the past. Caribou's three-story Sherman Hotel and the MacKenzie(formerly the Hetzer) Hotel in Nederland went up in smoke. The Antlers, in Nederland; the C&N, in Ward; the hotel at Corona, and others were dismantled, while Ward's Columbia Hotel stands vacant and in disrepair.

Eldora's century-old Gold Miner Hotel is the only one that survives. Owned by Scott Bruntjen and Carol Rinderknecht, it's open year around as a Bed and Breakfast. In addition, several contemporary lodging facilities welcome today's travelers to the Nederland and Peak to Peak areas.

It takes some imagination to picture the communities and their buildings in their heyday. Yet more and more people are committed to preserving their past. Author Forest Crossen was correct when he wrote that the Antler's Hotel register reflected the activities of the curious.

All we need to keep is our curiosity, and we can see them too.

BOOKS ON THE NEDERLAND AREA

Abele, Deborah Edge. *Metal Mining and Tourist Era Resources of Boulder County, National Register of Historic Places Multiple Property Listing.* Denver: Colorado Historical Society, 1989.

Becker, Isabel M. *Nederland, A Trip to Cloudland.* Denver: Scott Becker Press, 1989.

Bixby, A. *"History of Boulder County,"* in *History of Clear Creek and Boulder Valleys.* Chicago: O. L. Baskin & Co., 1880.

Bollinger, Edward T., and Frederick Bauer. *The Moffat Road.* Denver: Sage Books, 1962.

Boulder County Metal Mining Association. *Mining in Boulder County, Colorado.* Boulder: Boulder County Metal Mining Association, 1919.

Boulder County Parks and Open Space. *Exploring Boulder County.* Boulder: Boulder County Parks and Open Space Department, 1988.

Buchanan, John W., and Doris G. Buchanan. *The Story of Ghost Town Caribou.* Boulder: Boulder Publishing, Inc., 1957.

Cobb, Harrison S. *Prospecting Our Past: Gold, Silver, and Tungsten Mills of Boulder County.* Boulder: Book Lode, 1988.

Crossen, Forest. *The Switzerland Trail of America.* Boulder:

Pruett Publishing, 1962.

Dyni, Anne Quinby. *Back to the Basics, The Frontier Schools of Boulder County, 1860-1960.* Boulder: Book Lode, 1991.

Eson, Theo. *A Tale of Two Towns.* Nederland: Windmill Books & Gifts, 1986.

Kemp, Donald C., and John R. Langley. *Happy Valley, A Promoter's Paradise, Being an Historic Sketch of Eldora, Colorado and Its Environs.* Denver: Smith-Brooks Printing Company, 1945.

Kemp, Donald C. *Silver, Gold and Black Iron, A Story of the Grand Island Mining District of Boulder County, Colorado.* Denver: Sage Books, 1960.

Meier, Thomas J. *Ed Tangen, The Pictureman, A Photographic History of the Boulder Region, Early Twentieth Century.* Boulder: Boulder Creek Press, 1994.

Meyring, Geneva, *Nederland Then and Now.* Privately published, 1941.

Pettem, Silvia. *Excursions From Peak to Peak, Then and Now.* Longmont: Book Lode, 1997.

Pettem, Silvia. *Red Rocks to Riches, Gold Mining in Boulder County Then and Now.* Boulder: Stonehenge, 1980.

Rollins Pass Restoration Association. *The Moffat Road, A Self-guided Auto Tour.* Longmont: Rollins Pass Restoration Association (reprint by), 1996.

Smith, Duane A. *Silver Saga, The Story of Caribou, Colorado.* Boulder: Pruett Press, 1974.

Tripp, Betty J., *The Pioneers of Caribou, A Silver Ghost Town.* Detroit: Betty J. Tripp, 1996.

Weiss, Manuel. *Boulder County Historical Site Survey.* Denver: Colorado Historical Society, 1981.

INDEX

Adams, Governor Alva	48, 70.
Al's Place	111.
Albany Hotel, see Hotel McClancy.	
Anderson, Dr. Carrie	110.
Anderson, Frank J.	110.
Andrews, Darwin	vi.
Antler's Hotel	1, 20-22, 86, 91, 102-104, 119.
Arapaho Glacier	107, 111, 113.
Arapaho Pass	34, 54.
Arapaho Peak, see South Arapaho Peak.	
Arapaho Saddle	109.
Bailey, Neil	24.
Barker Dam	vi, 82, 83, 103.
Barker Meadows	vi, 20, 21.
Barker Reservoir (Lake Nederland)	20, 21, 82, 85, 103.
Barrett, Col. David	42.
Beach Block	98-100.
Beach's Addition	102.
Beach, Oran	2.
Beaver Creek	63.
Beaver Reservoir	79.
Bell, Jean	115.
Berthoud Pass	53.
Berthoud, Captain Edward L.	53, 55.
Binder's confectionery and stationery store	98.
Bixby, Amos	51.
Black Hawk	6-8, 12, 13, 63.
Black Hawk Indian Trail, see Ute trail.	
Blake's Hall	90.
Blake, C. W.	90, 92.
Bolton, Barbara	32, 50.
Boulder Canyon (Canon)	12, 21, 24, 63-65, 67, 83, 86, 90, 113.
Brainard Lake	80, 118.
Breed, Abel	10.
Brotherhood of Light cult	33.
Brown's Crossing	5.
Brown, Caroline	5.

Brown, Nathan	5.
Bruntjen, Scott	119.
Bucking Brown Trout Company	99.
Butterfield, D. A.	52.
C & N Hotel	73, 74, 76, 119.
C-BAR-E Stables	111.
Camp Audubon	80.
Cardinal	17, 81, 86, 100.
Caribou (City)	6-18, 24, 69, 82, 83, 119.
Caribou Ranch	5.
Caryl, Charles W.	32, 33, 46.
Catholic Daughters of America	104.
Caywood, Slim	84.
Central City	10-13, 47, 63.
Chaffee, Jerome B.	11.
Chapel of St. Rita, see St. Rita's Catholic Church.	
Childers, Robert	100, 101, 113, 114.
Clark, Jack	83.
Clifton, Robert B.	62.
Cochrane, Elizabeth (Nellie Bly)	65, 66.
Colorado House	30.
Colorado Power Company	82.
Columbia Hotel	73, 74, 76, 77, 119.
Community Presbyterian Church	87.
Connoran, Reverend James	15.
Cook, Charles A.	52, 53.
Corona	56, 58, 61, 62, 111, 119.
Cottage House	70.
Cox, Harry	112.
Cross, Isabel Hansen	49, 50.
Crossen, Forest	1, 56, 57, 76, 89.
Currens, Reverend	87.
Cutter, O. B.	10.
Dayton	5.
Devil's Slide Trestles	62.
DeVoss, William	100.
Dick's Corner Service Station	ii, 96.
Dick, Samuel B.	41.
Dixie Lodge	49, 50.
Dixie Siding	58.
Donald, William "Billy"	16.

Dunnagan, Francis	113, 114.
Dunnagan, Helen "D."	113, 114.
Durand store	112.
Eckel, Frank	67.
Eldora	ii, 2, 17, 19-50, 55, 72, 76, 82, 83, 85, 90, 94, 106-116.
Eldora Hotel	36, 46, 106, 117, 118.
Eldora Resort and Power Company	48.
Eldora Social & Civic Club	110.
Eldorado Springs	55.
Entwistle, Amos	35, 36.
Eureka House	24.
Fairhurst, Albert	74, 76.
Fairhurst, Emma	74-77.
Forest Lakes	62.
Forte, M.	111.
Fountain Restaurant	113, 114.
Fourth of July campground	44, 114.
Frontz, Dr.	84.
Garfield, President James A.	31.
Giben, Mrs.	31.
Gilfillan, John A.	23, 24, 36, 38.
Giteau, Charles J.	31.
Given, Mena	30-33, 46.
Glacier Lake	43, 70.
Gold Dirt, see Rollinsville.	
Gold Hill	3, 4, 51, 69, 70, 79.
Gold Hill station	70.
Gold Lake	80.
Gold Miner Hotel	ii, 29-34, 36, 41, 44-46, 94, 106-110, 113, 115, 116, 119.
Golden Gate Canyon	63.
Gordon Gulch	51.
Grand Island Mining District	4, 5.
Gross, William	111.
Hale, Carolyn Olsen	29.
Happy Valley (Eldorado)	19, 20.
Hardin, B. J.	38.
Hardin, Charles	38.
Hardin, Eliza McLauchland	38.
Harpel, Mayor William	111.

Harris, Bill	84.
Heller, Dr. Hilda	110.
Henderson, G. B.	79.
Hessie	38, 111.
Hetzer House (Hotel)	13-16, 33, 91, 93, 94, 103, 119.
Hetzer ranch	63.
Hetzer Saloon	14, 88, 92, 93.
Hetzer, J. W.	13.
Hetzer, Wesley	2, 16, 54.
Higgins and Foster saloon	25.
Hill, Nathaniel (Hill's Smelter)	7, 63.
Hodgson Transfer	101.
Holzhauser, Lois	20.
Hotel Columbia, see Columbia Hotel.	
Hub Store	92, 100.
Indian Peaks Wilderness	117.
Jackson, Helen Hunt	11, 12.
James Peak	111.
Jamestown	69, 79.
Jamieson, Louise	33, 94.
Jenny Lake	60.
Jyoti, Swami Amar	79
Kemp, Donald	2, 31, 37, 44, 93, 94.
Kemp, John	19.
Lacer House Hotel	91, 94.
Ladora	57.
Lake Eldora	2, 42, 47-49, 51, 63, 118.
Lake Eldora Inn (Pine Log Lodge)	49, 50.
Lake Ha Ha Tonka (Peterson Lake)	47.
Lake Nederland (see Barker Reservoir)	
Lakewood	90.
Lang, James A.	103.
Langcrest Hotel	103, 104.
Langley, John R. "Jack"	37, 44, 49.
LaPoint, Ann	37
LaPoint, Charles	37.
Lawrence, Mayor	84.
Leonard, J. Paul	112.
Lilly Stables	42, 111.
Lilly, Edna	50.

Lilly, Evelyn	32.
Lilly, Harold	32.
Lilly, John	42.
Little, Minnie	36.
Little, Robert H. B.	36.
Loach, William "Billy"	81, 82.
Lodge of the Pines	79.
Logue, William O.	8.
Long, "Shorty"	90, 92, 93.
Lost Lake	36, 111.
MacKenzie Hotel	15, 94, 103, 104, 119.
MacKenzie, John	94.
MacKenzie, Mollie	94.
Magnolia	63-66, 69, 76.
Martin, Dottie	115.
Martin, Fred	45.
Martin, Harold	114.
Martin, Harry	45.
Martin, Homer	45.
Martin, James	44.
Martin, Sarah	44-46, 106, 107.
Marysville	50.
Maupins Furniture store	94
Mayham Investment Company	25.
McClancy Hotel	71.
McClancy, Mrs. M. J.	71.
McClancy, Uriah	70.
McKenna, A. G.	81.
McKenzie's store	88, 92.
McKenzie, Colin	15, 16, 88, 94.
McNeil Haney vegetable wagon	111.
McRae Hotel	91-95.
Meyring, Geneva	85.
Middle Boulder	5, 6, 7, 10.
Middle Park	53, 54, 63, 67.
Mills & Mills	100.
Mills, N. M. "Fatty"	37, 38, 85, 92, 100.
Millsite Inn	80.
Mining Company Nederland of the Hague	10.
Mint Pool Hall	94, 95.
"Missouri Ann"	39.

Moffat Tunnel	57, 61, 118.
Moffat, David	11, 61.
Mont Alto	43, 70.
Monte Carlo	25, 35.
Morris, Annie	50.
Mountain House Hotel (Middle Boulder)	5, 13, 14.
Mountain People's Coop	92, 101.
Mrs. Martin's Restaurant	106, 107.
Murdock, R. C. "Dick"	93.
Nature's Own	101.
Nederland	ii, vi, 1, 5-22, 51, 81-106, 110, 111, 113, 117, 118.
Nederland City Hall	91.
Nederland Commercial Association	102.
Nederland Fish & Game Club	85, 86, 98.
Nederland House	15.
Nederland Mercantile	98.
Nederland Post Office	99.
Nederland Redman Band	90.
Nederland Rodeo	111.
Nederland Stone garage	91, 105.
Nederland Theatre (now Town Hall)	90, 91, 93.
Nederland Town Hall, see Nederland Theatre.	
Needle's Eye Tunnel	58, 60, 62.
Nellie Bly Gold Mining & Reduction Company	66.
Nellie Bly, see Elizabeth Cochrane	65.
Nelson, Helena	110.
Nolan, Bill	84.
O'Connor, Ben Hilliard	41.
Off Her Rocker Antiques	98.
Ogalalla Lodge	79.
Olsen's store	111.
Olsen, Olaf J.	29.
One World Cafe	97.
Paddock, L. C.	84.
Parsons, Martin	55.
Penrose Lodge	107, 109, 110.
Penrose, Elizabeth	107.
Perfect Tree	67, 68.
Peterson Lake	47, 48, 63.

Phebus, Glenn	50.
Pickel, John H.	15, 88, 92.
Pine Log Lodge (see Lake Eldora Inn).	
Pines Cafe	77.
Pioneer Saloon (not the Pioneer Inn)	98.
Planter's House	7, 8, 16.
Rainbow Lakes	107.
Randall, I. J.	29.
Randall, Jas. M.	29.
Range View Ranch	79.
Rearick, Elizabeth	107.
Reed, Mr.	42.
Richie's general store	16.
Rinderknecht, Carol	119.
Rodda, Agent	20, 47.
Rocky Mountain National Park	117.
Rogers Park	67.
Rollins Pass (South Boulder Pass)	41, 51, 42, 58, 59, 61, 63, 117.
Rollins, John Quincy Adams	51-55.
Rollinsville & Middle Park Wagon Road	55, 58, 62.
Rollinsville (Gold Dirt)	51, 53, 56, 61, 82.
Roose, Frank	21.
Roose, Mary	20.
Roose, Oscar	21.
Ross, Alice	46.
Rouse, Philip	111.
Russell, Green	3.
Sacred Mountain Ashram	79.
Salina	69.
Sargent's Boarding House	70.
Schmoll, Hazel	77, 79.
Scott's General Store	82, 98.
Seaman, Robert	65, 66.
Sewell, Jim	109, 111.
Sherman House	8, 9, 11, 16, 17, 119.
Silver Dollar Tavern	93, 95, 97, 105.
Sisson, A. F.	36.
Smith, Alice A.	29.
Smith, Lee	64.
Smith, Walter	64.
Souter, Dwight	115.

South Arapaho Peak	11, 44, 109, 113.
South Boulder Creek	56.
South Boulder Pass, see Rollins Pass.	
Spencer Mountain	23, 47, 50, 111.
Spruce Wye	58.
St. Rita's Catholic Church	104.
Stapp's Lake Lodge	78, 79.
Stapp, Bill	79.
Stapp, Isaac	79.
Stapp, John	79.
Stony Point Lodge	79.
Sturtevant, Joseph	34, 64.
Sugarloaf (Sugar Loaf) Mountain	51, 63.
Sulphide Flats	2, 51, 82, 83.
Sulphide Inn	70.
Sunset	41, 43, 70.
Sunshine	69.
Sunshine Canyon	51.
Sunshine Club (Society)	90.
Switzerland Park	63.
Tahosa Boy Scout Camp	79.
Tanner Brothers' grocery	93, 100, 101.
Tanner, Ira	82.
Tanner, Silas	82, 84.
Tanner, Wallace L.	81.
Thompson, Mrs. M. F.	74.
Tolland	56, 57, 61, 62.
Trollope House	16, 17.
Trollope, "Cap" George	91.
Trollope, Eugene R.	16.
Trollope, Mrs.	91, 92.
Tumblesom Lake	79.
Uncle Billy Donald Hotel	16.
Ute trail	2, 51, 54, 55, 63, 67.
Utica Hotel	70.
Valentine, John W.	86, 91.
Vendome Hotel	25, 26, 36.
Wall Street (Wallstreet)	32, 33, 69.
Ward	4, 12, 43, 44, 70-80, 117, 119.
Ward Congregational Church	72, 74.
Ward schoolhouse	72.

Ward, Calvin	4.
Werley, Peter	16.
Western Hotel	91.
Wheeler, H. N.	vi.
Wilkins, Mr. and Mrs. C.	8.
Wolf Tongue Square	97.
Woodland Lake	111.
Woodland Park Lodge	107.
Yankee Doodle Lake	55, 57, 58, 62.

Mines and mills

Anna Clara	66.
Bird's Nest	19.
Bonanza	19.
Caribou	7, 10, 11.
Caribou mill, see also Wolf Tongue mill.	10, 16, 81.
Clara	19.
Columbia	4, 74.
Enterprise mine and mill	19, 24, 39, 111.
Fourth of July	34-36, 44, 109, 111.
Gold Coin	19.
Graphic	76.
Grover Cleveland	23.
Kekionga	66.
Keystone mine and mill	64-66.
Little Stranger	23.
Mogul (Tunnel)	23, 36, 38, 41.
Mountain Lion	64.
Native Silver	16.
Poor Man	7.
Primos Mining & Milling Company	89, 102.
Quaker	102.
Revenge	36.
Sac and Fox	64.
Seven Thirty	16.
Somerset	23.
Spencer	16.
Terror	19.
Village Belle	19, 38.
Virginia	19.
Wolf Tongue mill	81, 86, 89.